150 Hungarian Recipes

(150 Hungarian Recipes - Volume 1)

Demi Decker

Content

150 Awesome Hungarian Recipes

***

---

1. Apple Strudel Easy!

Serving: 6 serving(s) | Prep: 20mins | Ready in:

Ingredients

- 1 egg
- 1 tablespoon water
- 2 apples, cord and sliced super thin on a mandolin
- 1/4 cup turbinado sugar
- 1 teaspoon cinnamon
- 1/4 teaspoon cardamom (optional)
- 1 lemon, juice
- 1 pinch salt
- 1/3 cup mixed nuts, dried fruit
- 1 teaspoon vanilla
- 1 tablespoon flour
- Topping
- 1 teaspoon sugar
- 1 puff pastry sheet, defrosted

Direction

- Preheat the oven to 375°F
- Beat the egg and water in a small bowl with a fork or whisk.
- Stir sugar cinnamon, lemon juice, salt, nuts, vanilla, and flour together.
- Mix in apples gently.
- Unfold the pastry sheet on a lightly floured surface. Roll the pastry sheet into a 16 x 12-inch rectangle. With the short side facing you, spoon the apple mixture onto the bottom half of the pastry sheet to within 1 inch of the edge. Roll up like a jelly roll. Place seam-side down onto a baking sheet lined with parchment. Tuck the ends under to seal. Brush the pastry with the egg mixture. Cut several slits in the top of the pastry. Sprinkle with 1 teaspoon sugar.
- Bake for 35 minutes or until the strudel is golden brown. Let the strudel cool on the baking sheet on a wire rack for 20 minutes.

Nutrition Information

- Calories: 320.6
- Saturated Fat: 4.8
- Fiber: 3.5
- Total Carbohydrate: 30.8
- Total Fat: 20.5
- Sodium: 191.4
- Sugar: 6.3
- Cholesterol: 35.2
- Protein: 5.8

---

2. Aunt Mary's Apple Cake

Serving: 8 serving(s) | Prep: 20mins | Ready in:

Ingredients

- 2 1/2-3 cups apples, peeled, cored, chopped
- 1 cup sugar
- 1 egg, beaten
- 1/2 cup unsalted butter, melted
- 1 1/2 cups flour
- 1 teaspoon baking soda
- 1 teaspoon salt
- 3/4 teaspoon cinnamon (or 1/2 teaspoon cinnamon and 1 teaspoon vanilla)
- 1/2 cup raisins
- 1/2 cup nuts, chopped (optional)

Direction

- Preheat oven to 350 degrees F.
- Sprinkle apples with sugar and let stand.

- Mix beaten egg and butter.
- Sift in flour, soda, salt and cinnamon and mix very well.
- Fold into apples and make sure the apples are well and evenly coated.
- Mix in raisins and, if desired, nuts.
- Note: we use raisins which have been soaked in bourbon.
- Note 2: If using regular raisins, make sure you plump them in warm water or rum or the like, then drain before adding.
- Place in a buttered 8" x 8" square baking dish or in a buttered Bundt pan and bake for about 50 minutes.
- Cool briefly on rack in pan; turn out of the pan and allow to cool to room temperature on a rack.

Nutrition Information

- Calories: 340.7
- Cholesterol: 53.8
- Saturated Fat: 7.5
- Sugar: 34.5
- Total Carbohydrate: 55.7
- Fiber: 2
- Protein: 3.7
- Total Fat: 12.4
- Sodium: 460.6

3. Baked Salty Sticks

Serving: 30 sticks | Prep: 10mins | Ready in:

Ingredients

- 1 cup butter
- 1 1/2 cups flour
- 1 cup cottage cheese
- 1 teaspoon baking soda
- 1 egg yolk
- 1 tablespoon salt
- sprinkling variations

- 2 tablespoons ground sumac or 2 tablespoons poppy seeds or 2 tablespoons sesame seeds or 1/4 cup grated cheese or 1 tablespoon ground oregano or 1 tablespoon garlic

Direction

- Mix butter with flour and baking soda.
- Add cottage cheese and mix well.
- Add more flour if too sticky.
- Roll out batter until 1/2-inch-thick and spread yolk over.
- (Putting batter into freezer for 10 minutes might help the stickiness too.).
- Sprinkle with salt, then sumac or poppy seeds, grated cheese or as you like.
- Cut into 1/2-inch-thick sticks.
- Bake at 350 until golden.

Nutrition Information

- Calories: 85.5
- Total Fat: 6.6
- Saturated Fat: 4.1
- Total Carbohydrate: 5
- Cholesterol: 23
- Protein: 1.6
- Sodium: 354.4
- Fiber: 0.2
- Sugar: 0.2

4. Balkan Poached Carp With Caraway Seeds

Serving: 4 , 4 serving(s) | Prep: 5mins | Ready in:

Ingredients

- 4 carp fillets (or other fish)
- 1 tablespoon butter
- 1 onion, finely diced
- 1 tablespoon caraway seed, bruised
- 2 tablespoons fresh chives, finely diced
- 1 lemon, juiced

- 1 cup dry white wine
- salt and pepper

Direction

- Heat the butter in the large frying pan. Add the caraway seeds and onions and fry until golden.
- Add the chives, lemon juice, and wine. Simmer 10 minutes.
- Add the fish and simmer 6 or 7 minutes. Flip and simmer another 3 or 4 minutes, or until fish is flaky.
- Remove fish, keep warm, and continue simmering to reduce sauce.
- Plate fish, season, and pour sauce on top.

Nutrition Information

- Calories: 94.9
- Protein: 0.9
- Sodium: 30
- Saturated Fat: 1.9
- Fiber: 1.6
- Sugar: 2.1
- Total Carbohydrate: 6.3
- Cholesterol: 7.6
- Total Fat: 3.2

5. Bar B Q Beef

Serving: 8-10 serving(s) | Prep: 15mins | Ready in:

Ingredients

- 5 lbs boneless chuck roast, lean
- 14 ounces chili sauce
- 1 quart dill pickle, including juice

Direction

- Put all ingredients into a large roaster and bake, covered @ 250 degrees for 11 hours.
- Do nothing for the first 6 hours.
- After 6 hours, stir every hour to break apart.

- Not necessary to add any other seasonings, not even salt.
- Before serving, mash or break apart with fork.
- Serve on hamburger buns.

Nutrition Information

- Calories: 787.4
- Sugar: 7.7
- Total Carbohydrate: 12.8
- Protein: 53.8
- Fiber: 3.8
- Cholesterol: 195.6
- Total Fat: 55.8
- Saturated Fat: 22.5
- Sodium: 1747.8

6. Beef Goulash With Dumplings Recipe

Serving: 4-6 serving(s) | Prep: 40mins | Ready in:

Ingredients

- Goulash
- 2 tablespoons extra virgin olive oil
- 4 cups onions, thinly sliced
- 1 tablespoon sugar
- 3 garlic cloves, minced
- 1 tablespoon caraway seed, toasted and ground
- 1 1/2 tablespoons sweet Hungarian paprika
- 1 teaspoon spicy Hungarian paprika
- 2 tablespoons minced fresh marjoram
- 1 teaspoon minced fresh thyme leave
- 1 bay leaf
- 3 tablespoons tomato paste
- 2 tablespoons balsamic vinegar
- 4 cups chicken stock
- 2 1/2 lbs chuck roast, cut into 2-inch cubes (remove excess fat)
- 1 teaspoon kosher salt
- 1/4 teaspoon fresh ground black pepper

- Dumplings
- 2 cups cake flour
- 2 teaspoons baking powder
- 1 teaspoon salt
- 3/4 cup milk
- 2 tablespoons melted butter

Direction

- In a large covered sauté pan, heat the olive oil and sauté the onions and sugar until caramelized. Add the garlic and caraway seed. Cook another minute.
- Add the sweet and spicy paprika, marjoram, thyme and bay leaf. Sauté another minute, until fragrant.
- Add the tomato paste. Deglaze with the vinegar and the stock and add the pieces of beef, salt and pepper. Bring to a boil, then lower to a simmer. Cover and cook until very tender, about 1 1/2 hours, stirring occasionally. Taste and adjust seasoning with salt and pepper.
- To prepare the dumplings, sift together the cake flour, baking powder and salt. Combine with the milk and melted butter, mixing lightly. Drop batter by teaspoonfuls into the simmering stew. Cover and cook for 15 minutes. Once you have covered the pan, do not uncover while the dumplings are cooking! In order for them to be light and fluffy, they must steam. If you uncover the pan, the steam will escape and the dumplings will boil instead. After 15 minutes, test the dumplings with a toothpick. If the toothpick comes out clean, the dumplings are done.

Nutrition Information

- Calories: 1306.1
- Sodium: 1875.9
- Sugar: 15.8
- Protein: 68.3
- Total Fat: 74
- Total Carbohydrate: 89.7
- Cholesterol: 224.5
- Saturated Fat: 29.1

- Fiber: 5.9

7. Beefy Eggplant (Aubergine) Soup

Serving: 6 serving(s) | Prep: 15mins | Ready in:

Ingredients

- 1 lb lean ground beef
- 2 medium onions, chopped
- 2 medium carrots, chopped
- 2 garlic cloves, minced
- 1 large eggplant, chopped
- 1 red sweet bell pepper, chopped
- 2 tablespoons paprika
- 1 tablespoon caraway seed
- 1 teaspoon dried thyme
- 1/2 teaspoon salt
- 1/2 teaspoon black pepper
- 5 cups beef stock
- 1 (28 ounce) can diced tomatoes
- 1 tablespoon tomato paste
- 2 cups small shell pasta
- 1/2 cup plain yogurt
- 1/4 cup chopped parsley

Direction

- In a Dutch oven over medium high heat cook the ground beef, breaking it up as it cooks.
- Drain off fat.
- Add the onions, carrots, garlic, eggplant, red pepper, paprika, caraway, thyme, salt and pepper.
- Cook for 10 minutes, stirring often.
- Add the stock, tomatoes, tomato puree and bring to a boil.
- Cover and reduce heat to a simmer, cooking for 30 minutes.
- Stir in the pasta and cook for another 15 minutes.
- To serve ladle into bowls and offer yogurt and parsley at the table.

Nutrition Information

- Calories: 375.8
- Protein: 25.7
- Saturated Fat: 4
- Sodium: 1235
- Fiber: 9.1
- Total Carbohydrate: 47.7
- Cholesterol: 51.8
- Total Fat: 10.2
- Sugar: 12.5

8. Blackened Chicken Fettuccine

Serving: 6 serving(s) | Prep: 8hours | Ready in:

Ingredients

- 1 tablespoon garlic powder
- 1 tablespoon onion powder
- 1 tablespoon dried thyme
- 1 tablespoon dried oregano
- 1 tablespoon paprika
- 1 tablespoon dried tarragon
- 1 tablespoon ground nutmeg
- 1 teaspoon salt
- 1 teaspoon ground red pepper
- 1/2 teaspoon black pepper
- 2/3 cup olive oil
- 1/2 cup Worcestershire sauce
- 5 boneless skinless chicken breasts
- 1/4 cup butter, melted
- 1 (12 ounce) package dry fettuccine
- 1/2 red bell pepper, cut into strips
- 1/2 yellow bell pepper, cut into strips
- 1/2 green bell pepper, cut into strips
- 2 stalks celery, sliced
- 1 medium onion, sliced
- 2 carrots, sliced
- 1 cup dry white wine
- 3/4 cup whipping cream
- 3 medium tomatoes, chopped

- 2 tablespoons water
- 1 teaspoon cornstarch
- fresh grated parmesan cheese

Direction

- Combine the first 12 ingredients in a zip lock bag; add the chicken and seal. Put in refrigerator and marinate for 8 hours, turning the bag occasionally.
- Remove the chicken from the bag; discard the marinade.
- Cook the chicken in the melted butter in a large skillet over medium high heat for 5 minutes on each side or until well browned; remove the chicken and reserve the drippings.
- Slice the chicken diagonally and set aside.
- Cook the pasta according to the package; drain well.
- Sauté all vegetables in the dripping for 4 minutes or until crisp tender.
- Add the wine, whipping cream, and tomatoes; simmer for 5 minutes.
- Combine the water and cornstarch; stir well and add to the vegetable mixture.
- Bring to a boil, and boil for 1 minute or until thickened, stirring constantly. Remove from the heat after it thickens; add the chicken and pasta toss well.
- Sprinkle with FRESH grated parmesan cheese.

Nutrition Information

- Calories: 822
- Sodium: 788.2
- Total Carbohydrate: 60.6
- Protein: 33.8
- Saturated Fat: 16.5
- Sugar: 9.2
- Cholesterol: 166
- Total Fat: 47.5
- Fiber: 5.7

9. Cabbage Roll Casserole With Just 5 Ingredients

Serving: 4-6 serving(s) | Prep: 25mins | Ready in:

Ingredients

- 1 lb ground beef
- 1 onion, sliced finely
- 1/8 teaspoon pepper
- salt
- 1 (10 3/4 ounce) can condensed tomato soup
- 1 soup can water
- 1/2 cup raw rice (or a tad more)
- 3 -4 cups cabbage, shredded

Direction

- Preheat oven to 350 degrees F. Have ready a 9- x 13-inch baking dish.
- Brown meat, breaking it up. Drain off the grease. Add salt, pepper, onion and rice as well as the tomato soup and can of water. Mix well.
- Put cabbage in the baking dish. Pour meat mixture over the cabbage but don't stir.
- Bake in preheated oven for approximately 1 hour. Near the end of the baking time, you may wish to stir contents and let bake a few more minutes.

Nutrition Information

- Calories: 399.1
- Total Carbohydrate: 34.7
- Cholesterol: 77.1
- Protein: 24.9
- Fiber: 3.4
- Sodium: 380.1
- Sugar: 9
- Total Fat: 17.6
- Saturated Fat: 6.8

10. Chicken Paprikas The Real Deal!

Serving: 6-8 serving(s) | Prep: 15mins | Ready in:

Ingredients

- 1 chopped onion
- 4 tablespoons shortening (can substitute you favorite cooking oil)
- 3 tablespoons paprika
- 1 teaspoon black pepper
- 1 teaspoon salt
- 4 -5 lbs chicken breasts
- 1 1/2 cups water
- 16 ounces sour cream
- dumplings
- 3 eggs
- 3 cups flour
- 1 teaspoon salt
- 1/2 cup water
- 1 teaspoon sour cream

Direction

- Brown onion in shortening or oil. Add seasonings and chicken.
- Brown chicken, then add water and cover. Simmer slowly until chicken is cooked and very tender.
- Remove chicken, cool and remove skin and bones.
- Add sour cream to pan drippings and mix well.
- Add chicken and dumplings, mix and heat together, and serve!
- Dumplings.
- Mix all ingredients together beat with a spoon.
- Drop batter by teaspoonful into boiling salted water. Cook about 7 to 10 minutes. Drain and rinse with cold water. Drain well, add to paprikash.

Nutrition Information

- Calories: 1050.9
- Fiber: 3.3

- Sugar: 1.6
- Total Carbohydrate: 55.3
- Cholesterol: 334.8
- Total Fat: 57
- Saturated Fat: 21.6
- Sodium: 1048.2
- Protein: 76

11. Chicken Paprikash #RSC

Serving: 1 pan, 4-6 serving(s) | Prep: 15mins | Ready in:

Ingredients

- 1/4 lb bacon
- 1 cup shallot, peeled and sliced
- 2 garlic cloves, minced
- 2 boneless skinless chicken breasts, cut into 1/2-inch slices
- 1 cup baby carrots, sliced
- 1 cup chicken broth
- 1/3 cup dry white wine
- 2 tablespoons lemon juice
- 1/4 cup pomegranate molasses
- 1 (1 ounce) package Hidden Valley Original Ranch Dressing Mix
- 1 1/2 cups Greek yogurt
- 1 tablespoon paprika, smoked, hot
- 1 teaspoon nutmeg, grated
- 1 (14 ounce) can artichoke bottoms, drained and quartered

Direction

- Fry bacon in a heavy, non-stick skillet until crisp. Remove with a slotted spoon and drain on paper towels; crumble and set aside. Discard all but 2 tablespoons of the drippings. Stir shallots and garlic into pan. Stir-fry over medium heat until shallots are soft.
- Push shallots to edge of pan. Add chicken. Stir-fry until chicken is nicely browned. Add carrots, chicken broth, wine, lemon juice and molasses. Cover and simmer over low heat for 15 minutes.

- Sprinkle Hidden Valley Mix over chicken, then stir in the crumbled bacon, yogurt, paprika, nutmeg and artichoke bottoms. Simmer for 3 more minutes. Taste and add salt if desired.

Nutrition Information

- Calories: 321.3
- Sodium: 616.9
- Fiber: 7.1
- Total Carbohydrate: 22.9
- Protein: 21.9
- Total Fat: 15.3
- Sugar: 3.4
- Cholesterol: 57
- Saturated Fat: 4.9

12. Chicken And Dumplings With Herbed Broth

Serving: 4 serving(s) | Prep: 30mins | Ready in:

Ingredients

- 3 cups self rising flour, plus
- 1 tablespoon self rising flour, in all
- 1 teaspoon pepper
- 3 lbs chicken legs or 3 lbs chicken thighs (I use chicken tenders)
- 1/4 cup olive oil
- 1 onion, chopped
- 2 cloves garlic, minced
- 3 (14 1/2 ounce) cans chicken broth (I use homemade)
- 2 tablespoons chopped fresh basil
- 2 tablespoons chopped fresh thyme
- 1 tablespoon chopped fresh rosemary
- 1/2 teaspoon grated fresh lemon rind
- 2 tablespoons lemon juice
- 1 cup whipping cream
- 1/4 cup sour cream

Direction

- Combine 1 cup flour and pepper dredge chicken in flour mixture.
- Heat oil over medium heat and brown chicken add more oil if needed remove chicken save drippings.
- Add onion and garlic cook till tender.
- Add 1 T. flour cook for 1-minute stirring constantly slowly add broth add fresh herbs, lemon rind, lemon juice.
- Bring to boil return chicken cover and reduce heat simmer 30 minutes.
- Remove chicken keep warm.
- Combine 2 cups flour and whipping cream stir with a fork pat into 2-inch balls handling as little as possible.
- Bring broth to boil add dumplings cover reduce heat simmer 7 to 10 minutes or till firm in center.
- Remove from heat add sour cream.

Nutrition Information

- Calories: 1398.2
- Total Fat: 82.6
- Sugar: 3.1
- Total Carbohydrate: 78.5
- Cholesterol: 371.6
- Saturated Fat: 29.6
- Sodium: 2530.8
- Fiber: 3.5
- Protein: 80.1

13. Chocolate Marzipan Slices (Hungarian Candies)

Serving: 1 tray, 24 serving(s) | Prep: 25mins | Ready in:

Ingredients

- 7 ounces almond paste
- 2 (1 ounce) semi-sweet chocolate baking squares, melted cooled
- 1/4 cup chopped almonds
- confectioners' sugar

Direction

- Mix almond paste (which has been grated, using a box grater), chocolate and almonds.
- Knead on surface sprinkled with 1-2 tablespoons confectioners' sugar until of uniform colour consistency.
- Shape into 6" long roll; roll in confectioners' sugar.
- Wrap in plastic wrap; refrigerate at least 12 hours.
- Cut roll into 1/4" slices = 24 candies.

Nutrition Information

- Calories: 60
- Sodium: 5.9
- Total Carbohydrate: 6
- Protein: 1.2
- Total Fat: 3.9
- Saturated Fat: 0.7
- Fiber: 0.7
- Sugar: 4.5
- Cholesterol: 0

14. Crackling Biscuits

Serving: 72 biscuits | Prep: 15mins | Ready in:

Ingredients

- 1 lb cracklings, ground
- 6 cups flour
- 1 tablespoon baking powder
- 1 tablespoon salt
- 2 eggs
- 1/4 pint sour cream
- 1/2 cup your favorite wine (I use chardonnay)
- 1 egg yolk
- 1/2 cup cream

Direction

- Preheat oven to 300°F.

- In large bowl mix together cracklings, flour, baking powder, and salt.
- In a separate bowl whisk together the eggs, sour cream, and wine.
- Make a well in the center of the flour mixture and pour the egg mixture into it.
- Gradually combined the two mixtures.
- On a flour surface roll dough to 3/4-inch thickness and cut with a 2 1/2-3-inch cookie cutter.
- Place biscuit rounds on a greased cookie sheet.
- In a small bowl whisk together the egg yolk and cream.
- Brush the tops of biscuits with cream mixture.
- Bake for 20-25 minutes.

Nutrition Information

- Calories: 50.4
- Total Fat: 1.1
- Saturated Fat: 0.6
- Cholesterol: 11
- Protein: 1.4
- Sodium: 115.8
- Fiber: 0.3
- Sugar: 0.1
- Total Carbohydrate: 8.2

15. Cream Stuffed Bell Peppers

Serving: 5 serving(s) | Prep: 30mins | Ready in:

Ingredients

- 1/2 lb ground beef
- 1/2 lb ground pork
- 1 medium onion, diced
- 1 cup rice, washed (not instant)
- 1 tablespoon salt
- 1 tablespoon sweet paprika
- 1/2 teaspoon pepper
- 1 (8 ounce) can Campbell's condensed tomato soup
- 8 -9 medium green peppers
- 1/2 pint heavy cream

Direction

- Prepare peppers by cutting off tops.
- Remove seeds and scrape insides with teaspoon.
- Wash peppers.
- Mince and lightly brown onion in small amount of oil, add paprika at end of browning.
- Pour this in a large bowl and mix with meat, rice and seasoning.
- Fill green peppers with mixture of rice and meat.
- Place peppers in deep pot; pour on tomato soup and enough water to cover peppers (sometimes I will add two cans for richer gravy).
- Simmer for 1 hour or until rice is cooked; when rice is soft peppers are done.
- Add heavy cream to liquid after peppers are finished and serve. (Do not boil after cream is added).
- When serving cut meatball and place sauce on top.

Nutrition Information

- Calories: 616.2
- Sugar: 9.4
- Cholesterol: 138.7
- Saturated Fat: 17.5
- Fiber: 5.2
- Protein: 26.4
- Total Fat: 34.9
- Sodium: 1735.7
- Total Carbohydrate: 50.4

16. Crock Pot Hungarian Beef Goulash

Serving: 4 serving(s) | Prep: 20mins | Ready in:

Ingredients

- 1 onion, sliced
- 3 carrots, cut into small pieces
- 1/4 cup all-purpose flour
- 2 teaspoons dried marjoram
- 1 1/2 teaspoons salt
- 3/4 teaspoon pepper
- 2 lbs beef stew meat, cut into 1 inch cubes
- 1/2 cup beef broth
- 1/4 cup red wine
- 1/4 cup tomato paste
- 4 teaspoons ground paprika
- 2 garlic cloves, minced
- 2 tablespoons sour cream
- 8 ounces egg noodles

Direction

- Place onions and carrots in crock pot.
- Combine next four ingredients; toss beef with this mixture and add to crock pot.
- Combine broth, wine, tomato paste, paprika and garlic; pour over beef.
- Cover crock pot and cook 7-8 hours on low.
- When stew is ready cook noodles and transfer to platter.
- Stir sour cream into stew.
- Top noodles with stew.

Nutrition Information

- Calories: 1111.3
- Sodium: 1268
- Fiber: 5.5
- Total Carbohydrate: 59.6
- Cholesterol: 286.7
- Total Fat: 62.8
- Saturated Fat: 24.8
- Sugar: 6.7
- Protein: 71.5

17. Crock Pot Hungarian Goulash

Serving: 6 serving(s) | Prep: 20mins | Ready in:

Ingredients

- 2 lbs beef stew meat, cut into 1 inch cubes
- 1 large onion, sliced
- 1 clove garlic, minced
- 1/2 cup ketchup
- 2 tablespoons Worcestershire sauce
- 1 tablespoon brown sugar
- 2 teaspoons salt
- 2 teaspoons paprika
- 1/2 teaspoon dry mustard
- 1 cup water
- 1/4 cup flour

Direction

- Place meat in crockpot and cover with sliced onion.
- Combine garlic, ketchup, Worcestershire sauce, sugar, salt, paprika and mustard. Stir in water, mix well, and pour over meat.
- Cover and cook on low for 8 to 10 hours.
- Turn control to high.
- Dissolve flour in a small amount of cold water and stir into meat mixture.
- Cook on high for 10 to 15 minutes or until slightly thickened.
- Serve over noodles or rice.

Nutrition Information

- Calories: 258.8
- Total Fat: 7.1
- Saturated Fat: 3
- Sodium: 1178
- Fiber: 0.9
- Sugar: 8.5
- Total Carbohydrate: 15.6
- Cholesterol: 96.8
- Protein: 34.2

18. Csirke Paprikash / Chicken Paprikash

Serving: 4-6 serving(s) | Prep: 20mins | Ready in:

Ingredients

- 1 whole chicken
- 1 large onion
- 2 tablespoons oil
- 1 tablespoon paprika
- 2 red peppers
- 1 large tomatoes
- 1 teaspoon salt
- 1/4 teaspoon pepper
- 1 cup sour cream (Opcional)

Direction

- Cut up chicken you can keep skin on or remove according to preference or diet. My Mom would always season the chicken with salt and let it sit for a while in a colander to lose any extra water that might remain after washing.
- Chop onion very fine and sauté in a heavy pot or Dutch oven until it softens then add paprika be very careful not to burn the paprika because it will taste bitter.
- I remove the onion/paprika mixture and brown the chicken on high heat adding oil if needed. Once browned I return the onion mix to the pot, season with salt and pepper, turn down the heat, cover and let cook for about 15 minutes. Dice tomato and pepper leaving a few pepper rings for garnish add them to chicken cover and continue cooking stirring occasionally for about 40 to 60 minutes. I do not add water as the chicken releases enough of its own juices but if you find it to be to dry add water.
- Many like to add sour cream (I prefer mine without) before serving, just mix it in and let it cook long enough to warm up the sauce.

Nutrition Information

- Calories: 949.3
- Saturated Fat: 23.6
- Sugar: 5.6
- Cholesterol: 269.1
- Protein: 60.7
- Total Fat: 72.3
- Sodium: 844.2
- Fiber: 2.9
- Total Carbohydrate: 12.7

19. Easy Caramel Rugelach (Jayne Cohen)

Serving: 34 rugelach | Prep: 30mins | Ready in:

Ingredients

- PASTRY
- 2 1/3 cups unbleached all-purpose flour
- 1/4 teaspoon salt
- 3 tablespoons brown sugar, granulated
- 8 ounces cream cheese, chilled and cut into bits (1 cup)
- 1 cup unsalted butter, chilled and cut into bits (2 sticks or 1/2 pound)
- 1/4 cup sour cream
- 1 teaspoon vanilla extract
- FILLING
- 1/2 cup light brown sugar, granulated or packed
- 1 3/4-2 cups packaged caramels, such as Kraft's, cut into small bits (about 12 ounces)
- 1 cup pecans, coarsely chopped

Direction

- Make the pastry. In a food processor, mix the flour, salt, and brown sugar. Add the cream cheese, butter, sour cream, and vanilla and pulse just until the mixture begins to form a ball around the blades. Do not overprocess. Transfer the dough to a work surface and knead lightly and quickly into a smooth, compact roll. (Or prepare manually: In a large bowl, quickly mix together the cream cheese, butter, sour cream, and vanilla until well blended. Gradually add the flour, salt, and sugar. Knead the mixture lightly until thoroughly combined and smooth.).

- Divide the dough into 4 equal parts. Put each piece between two sheets of wax paper and flatten into a large oblong using the palm of your hand. If necessary, refrigerate briefly until the dough is firm enough to roll.
- Work with one oblong at a time, keeping the others refrigerated. Roll the oblong between the wax paper into a 12-by-7-inch rectangle, about 1/8 inch thick. Leaving the dough in the wax paper, refrigerate for at least 4 hours or up to 2 days. Repeat with the other 3 rectangles.
- Loosen the wax paper from both sides of the dough. (The paper becomes pressed into the dough with rolling and will be difficult to remove after you cut the dough unless it has been loosened first.) Place the dough rectangle back down on a sheet of the wax paper, and sprinkle it all over with 2 tablespoons brown sugar. Now cut the rectangle in half. You should have two 6-by-7-inch sections. Cut each section into 4 equal strips, giving you 8 in all. Leaving a 1/2-inch border, place some caramel pieces and pecans over each dough strip (be generous, the more caramels, the more luscious the taste). If your caramels are soft enough, press the pieces with your fingertips to flatten them. You'll get a smoother, tighter roll. Roll each strip up tightly, jelly-roll fashion, and place seam side down, about I inch apart, on a baking sheet lined with parchment. (If the dough becomes too soft to work with during the rolling or filling, place it on a lined cookie sheet in the freezer until firm again.) Refrigerate the prepared rugelach while you make rugelach with the rest of the dough. The prepared rugelach should be refrigerated for at least 30 minutes before you bake them.
- Preheat the oven to 375°F Bake in the middle of the oven for about 20 minutes, or until pale golden. If necessary, adjust the pans during baking so the rugelach cook evenly. Transfer

the pan to a rack and let the rugelach cool completely. Remove the rugelach carefully with a thin-bladed spatula. Store the rugelach in airtight containers for up to 4 days.

Nutrition Information

- Calories: 145.3
- Saturated Fat: 5.3
- Total Carbohydrate: 11.6
- Cholesterol: 22.4
- Protein: 1.8
- Total Fat: 10.5
- Sodium: 40.4
- Fiber: 0.5
- Sugar: 4.5

20. Eggs Baked In Potatoes

Serving: 6 serving(s) | Prep: 30mins | Ready in:

Ingredients

- 6 large potatoes
- 4 tablespoons butter
- 1⁄4 cup milk, hot
- 1⁄4 teaspoon salt
- 1⁄4 teaspoon pepper
- 6 eggs
- 1⁄2 cup cheese, shredded

Direction

- Bake the potatoes.
- Scoop out the pulp, after cutting a thin slice from the length of the potato.
- Mash pulp to a creamy fluff with butter, hot milk, salt and pepper.
- Fill potato shells, leaving a dent in the middle of each to hold a raw egg.
- Break 1 or 2 eggs into each potato.
- Cover with cheese.
- Bake at 400°F for 10 minutes until the egg is firm and cheese is browned.

Nutrition Information

- Calories: 461.4
- Protein: 16
- Total Fat: 15.4
- Fiber: 8.1
- Sugar: 3.1
- Saturated Fat: 8.2
- Sodium: 353.6
- Total Carbohydrate: 66.2
- Cholesterol: 213.8

21. Elizabeth Báthory Stir Fry

Serving: 2 serving(s) | Prep: 15mins | Ready in:

Ingredients

- 1 yellow pepper
- 1 red pepper
- 2 tomatoes
- 400 g turkey breast
- 2 tablespoons paprika
- 1/2 tablespoon dried garlic
- 1 tablespoon black pepper (ground)
- 1 tablespoon cinnamon
- 1/2 teaspoon salt
- 2 tablespoons tomato sauce or 2 tablespoons ketchup or 2 tablespoons tomato concentrate
- 1 cup water
- 120 g white rice
- 1 1/2 tablespoons butter

Direction

- Chop the peppers and tomatoes and sprinkle them with all spices. Set aside.
- Dice the turkey, being careful not to chop it too thinly. Mix with the veggies and leave the mix be.
- Boil the rice. When it's done, put the butter into the frying pan and melt it. When the butter is nice and melted, put all the veggies and meat in and stir.
- Fry the mix for about 7-10 minutes, and when the meat is visibly fried white, pour one cup of water into the mix. Stir the mix and let it be for another 5 minutes.
- Watch your mix, as the water reduces and after a while you should see the liquid hit the point where it covers the meat only halfway. Add the tomato condiment of choice.
- At that point add the boiled rice and mix well. Serve while hot.

Nutrition Information

- Calories: 722.5
- Saturated Fat: 9.7
- Fiber: 10.8
- Sugar: 7.2
- Total Carbohydrate: 73.8
- Protein: 52.4
- Total Fat: 24.7
- Sodium: 878.3
- Cholesterol: 152.9

22. Esterhazy Torte/Esterhazyschnitten/Almond Meringue Slices

Serving: 8 slces | Prep: 1hours | Ready in:

Ingredients

- Cake layers
- 1/2 cup hazelnuts (2 1/2 ounces, toasted and peeled)
- 1/2 cup sliced almonds (2 ounces, natural or blanched)
- 1/4 cup confectioners' sugar
- 5 large egg whites, at room temperature
- 1/2 cup granulated sugar
- Kirsch Buttercream
- 1 cup milk, divided

- 2 tablespoons cornstarch
- 2/3 cup granulated sugar
- 2 large egg yolks
- 1 cup unsalted butter (2 sticks, at cool room temperature, cut into small pieces)
- 2 tablespoons kirsch or 2 tablespoons cognac or 2 tablespoons golden rum
- Assembly
- 1/4 cup warm apricot jam or 1/4 cup apricot glaze
- faux fondant (see recipe below)
- 1 ounce bittersweet chocolate, melted
- 1/2 cup sliced almonds, toasted (for garnish)
- Small-Batch Faux Fondant Icing
- 1 cup confectioners' sugar, sifted
- 1 tablespoon warm water
- 2 teaspoons warm water
- 2 teaspoons light corn syrup

Direction

- To make the nut layers: Position a rack in the centre of the oven and pre-heat to 350° F. Butter a 17 x 11 inch jelly-roll pan; line the bottom and sides with parchment paper. [Cut slashes in the corners of the paper to help them fold neatly.].
- In a food processor fitted with the metal blade, process the hazelnuts, almonds, and confectioners' sugar until the nuts are finely chopped. [Or buy ground nuts.] In a large grease-free bowl, whip the egg whites until soft peaks form. Gradually add the granulated sugar and whip until stiff, shiny peaks form. Fold in the nuts.
- Spread the batter evenly in the prepared jelly-roll pan. Bake until golden brown, about 20 minutes. Unmold the cake onto a cutting board, peel off the parchment paper, and cool completely. The, trim the edges to even out, and cut the cake vertically into six 2 ¾ -inch-wide strips.
- Buttercream filling: Heat ¼ cup of the milk in a heavy-bottomed saucepan. Add the cornstarch and whisk to dissolve. Whisk in the sugar, then the egg yolks. Add the remaining ¾ cup of milk and whisk over

medium heat until very thick. Remove from the heat and transfer to a bowl set in a larger bowl of ice water; stir and cool. Using a hand-held electric mixer, add the butter, one tablespoon at a time, then add the kirsch.
- Faux Fondant Icing: Combine all the ingredients in a small sauce pan; stir over low heat until the glaze is barely warm, 92° to 95°F. Use immediately.
- Assembly: Place the best-looking nut layer on a wire rack, smooth side up. Spread this layer with warm apricot jam and let stand for about 15 minutes. Pour warm fondant icing over the jam letting any excess drip over the sides. Pipe four thin line of chocolate about ¾ inch apart along the entire length of the icing. To make a feathered effect, at one-inch intervals, draw a wooden toothpick in straight line perpendicular to the long lines of chocolate. Let stand until the icing and chocolate are firm.
- Meanwhile, place 1 nut layer on a cutting board; spread it with about 3 tablespoons of the buttercream. Repeat with the remaining layers, ending with the buttercream. Spread the remaining buttercream around the sides of the cake. Press sliced almonds onto the sides. Top with the iced layer. Refrigerate uncovered for at least one hour prior to slicing.

Nutrition Information

- Calories: 589.3
- Protein: 7.9
- Sodium: 60.5
- Fiber: 2.3
- Total Carbohydrate: 63.2
- Total Fat: 36.1
- Saturated Fat: 16.5
- Sugar: 53.3
- Cholesterol: 111.4

23. Fahdreiteh Chicken

Serving: 6 serving(s) | Prep: 24hours20mins | Ready in:

Ingredients

- 1 1/2 kg chicken pieces
- 1 1/2 heads garlic, crushed
- 1 tablespoon sweet paprika
- 3 teaspoons sea salt
- 4 tablespoons vegetable oil
- 1/2 teaspoon soy sauce

Direction

- Clean the chicken well and wipe dry.
- Prepare a marinade with the crushed garlic, paprika, sea salt, salt, oil and soy sauce.
- Let the mixture rest of 20 minutes.
- Place the chicken pieces in the marinade and turn to cover well.
- Cover the dish and place in the refrigerator for 24 hours (or 16, at least).
- Bake uncovered for approximately one hour at 250 degrees Celsius.

Nutrition Information

- Calories: 643.5
- Saturated Fat: 12
- Sodium: 1369
- Total Carbohydrate: 5.6
- Protein: 47.7
- Total Fat: 46.9
- Fiber: 0.7
- Sugar: 0.3
- Cholesterol: 187.5

24. Favorite Chicken Paprika

Serving: 4 serving(s) | Prep: 5mins | Ready in:

Ingredients

- 2 tablespoons unsalted butter
- 1 tablespoon vegetable oil
- 1 lb boneless chicken tenderloins
- 2 medium onions, chopped
- 2 tablespoons sweet Hungarian paprika
- salt, to taste
- 2/3 cup crushed tomatoes
- hot buttered egg noodles
- sour cream (I prefer Breakstone's Light)

Direction

- Preheat the oven to 300 degrees.
- In a casserole dish, heat the butter and oil on the stovetop over medium-high heat.
- Add the chicken tenderloins and cook until browned on all sides, then remove to a plate.
- Add the onions to the casserole, reduce heat to medium and cook (stirring often) until they're golden brown.
- Stir in the paprika and cook for an additional minute.
- Return the chicken to the casserole, season with salt and cover tightly.
- Bake for 20-30 minutes, until chicken is cooked through.
- Add the tomato puree, stir and cook for 5 more minutes, or until puree is heated through.
- Serve over hot buttered egg noodles with a dollop of sour cream.

Nutrition Information

- Calories: 254.7
- Sugar: 4.3
- Cholesterol: 81.1
- Total Fat: 11.6
- Saturated Fat: 4.7
- Sodium: 175.2
- Fiber: 2.7
- Total Carbohydrate: 10.2
- Protein: 27.8

25. Fish Baked In A Dough Jacket

Serving: 4 , 4 serving(s) | Prep: 1hours | Ready in:

Ingredients

- 1 kg whole fish (choose a flavorful fish like trout)
- salt and pepper
- 1 lemon, cut into wedges, to serve
- 225 g white flour, sifted
- 1 1/2 ml salt
- 7 g active dry yeast
- 1 egg
- 60 ml warm water
- 60 ml milk

Direction

- If needed, scale and gut fish. Cut off head behind gills/dorsal fins, and cut off the tail.
- Wipe fish dry with a paper towel. Rub inside and out with salt and pepper and put in the refrigerator.
- Put flour, salt, and yeast in a large mixing bowl and stir to combine.
- Whisk egg, milk and water in a separate bowl. Add about half to the flour bowl and knead to make a soft dough. Add a little more liquid if needed.
- Move dough to a floured work surface and knead until smooth. Cut into two pieces, one a little larger than the other.
- Roll the smaller piece so that it is larger than the fish, with about 2 cm (1 1/2 in) border on all sides. Place on a greased baking sheet and put the fish on top, centered.
- Roll the larger piece of dough until it is large enough to drape over the fish and still have 2 cm (1 1/2 in) of border. Don't put it on the fish yet.
- Apply some warm water on the border area of the lower piece of dough. Place top dough on the fish and press the border areas together to form a seal.
- Allow to rise for 30 minutes.
- Brush the remaining egg/milk/water onto the dough to form a glaze. Bake 30 minutes at 180 C (350 F).

Nutrition Information

- Calories: 241.9
- Saturated Fat: 0.8
- Fiber: 2.4
- Sugar: 0.6
- Total Carbohydrate: 45.8
- Protein: 8.7
- Total Fat: 2.5
- Sodium: 205.6
- Cholesterol: 48.5

26. Fish Baked With Sour Cream

Serving: 4-6 serving(s) | Prep: 25mins | Ready in:

Ingredients

- 1 lb fish fillet, patted dry (I use firm white fish)
- 4 ounces sliced mushrooms
- 1 small onion, chopped
- 1 tablespoon butter
- 1/2 teaspoon thyme
- 1/4-1/2 teaspoon salt
- 1/4-1/2 teaspoon pepper (can use either white or black)
- 1/2 cup sour cream, at room temperature (if using light sour cream, bring to room temperature and stir well)
- 3 -5 tablespoons grated or shredded parmesan cheese
- 2 tablespoons dry breadcrumbs
- paprika (for garnish)
- chopped parsley (for garnish)

Direction

- Put fish into a rectangular baking dish (approx. 12 x 7. 5 x 2), sprayed lightly with a baking spray.

- Preheat oven to 350 degrees Fahrenheit.
- Over medium to medium-high heat, melt butter in a skillet large enough to hold mushrooms and onions.
- Sauté mushrooms and onions about 3 minutes, until mushrooms are golden, sprinkling with thyme when about halfway through.
- Spoon mushroom and onion mix over fish and sprinkle lightly with salt and pepper.
- Sprinkle about 1 1/2 T parmesan (or to taste) over the mushroom and onion mixture.
- Mix remaining cheese into sour cream.
- Spread sour cream over mushroom/onion mixture, using a spatula.
- Sprinkle with bread crumbs.
- Bake uncovered for about 25- 30 minutes, or until fish flakes with fork.
- Sprinkle with parsley and paprika and serve.

Nutrition Information

- Calories: 243.1
- Total Fat: 10.9
- Sugar: 2.6
- Cholesterol: 88.2
- Protein: 29.5
- Saturated Fat: 6
- Sodium: 366.3
- Fiber: 0.8
- Total Carbohydrate: 6.1

27. Fluffy Pogaca (Peasant Buns)

Serving: 15 serving(s) | Prep: 1hours | Ready in:

Ingredients

- For dough
- 1/4 cup milk, WARMED
- 1 tablespoon sugar
- 1 tablespoon instant yeast
- 4 cups flour
- 1/2 cup vegetable oil
- 1 teaspoon salt

- 3/4 cup mineral water
- For filling
- 1/2 bunch parsley
- 1 1/2 cups feta cheese
- For topping
- 1 egg yolk, beaten
- 2 tablespoons poppy seeds

Direction

- Mix sugar and yeast with milk.
- Combine flour, oil, salt, and mineral water in large bowl.
- Add milk mixture and mix well. You can add a little more flour or mineral water if either of them is not enough. You should have a pliable and non-sticky dough.
- Cover with moist cloth and let rest for 45 minutes.
- Chop the parsley and mix it with cheese.
- PREHEAT oven to 350 degrees F or 180 degrees Celsius.
- Take a small piece of dough and flatten with your hands.
- Put a teaspoon of cheese mixture on it, close up folding the edges upwards like a bundle, and repeat with remaining dough.
- Place a parchment paper on a baking sheet and place the pogacas on it.
- The FOLDED side of pogacas should be at the bottom to have a ball shape.
- Coat each with egg yolk and a sprinkle of poppy seeds.
- Bake about 30 minutes, or until they get golden.

Nutrition Information

- Calories: 243
- Protein: 6.4
- Sodium: 326.4
- Fiber: 1.2
- Sugar: 1.7
- Total Carbohydrate: 27.7
- Cholesterol: 26.5
- Total Fat: 11.8

- Saturated Fat: 3.5

28. Garlic Schnitzel

Serving: 4-6 serving(s) | Prep: 30mins | Ready in:

Ingredients

- 4 -6 pork cutlets (pounded to 1/8 inch thickness)
- milk
- 3 garlic cloves
- salt or seasoning salt
- flour
- 2 -3 eggs
- breadcrumbs
- oil (for frying)

Direction

- Place unpounded pork cutlets in casserole pan, trying to not overlap meat. Use a garlic press to evenly distribute garlic over each piece of meat, and pour enough milk over the top to cover the meat and garlic. Let it sit in your refrigerator for at least an hour, or overnight for best flavor.
- Remove meat carefully, trying to keep garlic pieces on top, and put them into plastic wrap or storage bag to pound garlic into the pork with the flat side of a meat tenderizer. (Using a plastic bag helps keep the garlic in place and allows the meat to stretch). When removing the pounded pork, sprinkle both sides with salt or seasoned salt, and put onto a large plate.
- Prepare the breading step by tearing 2 square sheets of aluminum foil for the flour and breadcrumbs, and froth 2-3 eggs in large, flat bowl (or pie pan). Add some salt to the egg mixture. In an assembly line style, place aluminum foil square of flour (about 1-2 cups), then the bowl of mixed eggs, and finally the bread crumbs (2 cups). Have a large plate or cookie sheet ready to place the breaded meat.

Dip the pounded, salted pork into the flour (shaking off excess), then into egg, and using a fork, lift out of the egg mixture and let excess egg drip off, and place into breadcrumbs. The foil is good to use, so that you can lift the sides to shake on the breadcrumbs without using your fingers. Throw away the leftover flour and breadcrumbs with the foil.

- Heat oil in deep frying pan, making sure the oil is at least 1 inch thick in pan. Oil is ready when you drop a bread crumb into it, and it fizzes up to the top. Fry the meat on each side (about 2 minutes each side) until golden brown and place onto plate lined with paper towels.
- For the special "tartar sauce," mix equal amounts of mayonnaise and sour cream, and squirt some mustard into it. You can add salt and pepper to taste, too. This is a great dip for the garlic Schnitzel. Enjoy!

Nutrition Information

- Calories: 40.1
- Total Fat: 2.5
- Saturated Fat: 0.8
- Sugar: 0.2
- Total Carbohydrate: 0.9
- Cholesterol: 105.8
- Sodium: 35.4
- Fiber: 0.1
- Protein: 3.3

29. Grandpa's Hungarian Kolacky

Serving: 64 cookies | Prep: 30mins | Ready in:

Ingredients

- 1 cup butter or 1 cup margarine, softened
- 2 (3 ounce) packages cream cheese, softened
- 2 cups all-purpose flour

- assorted baking jelly or pie filling (my favorites are apricot, poppy seed, almond, and raspberry)
- powdered sugar

Direction

- Combine butter and cream cheese completely, add flour and mix well.
- Divide dough into 4 balls; wrap each in plastic wrap and chill 24 hours.
- Roll out each ball (on floured surface) to 1/8". (Be sure to keep them thin, as this keeps them "light!")
- Cut out silver-dollar sized cookies; place on ungreased cookie sheets.
- Drop 1/2 teaspoon jelly in center of each cookie and bake at 350* for 7-8 min. (Just until edges begin to brown.) I always bake the cookies flat; however, the edges may be pinched or rolled together as well!
- Lightly sift powdered sugar over cookies and serve.

Nutrition Information

- Calories: 48.9
- Total Fat: 3.8
- Saturated Fat: 2.4
- Total Carbohydrate: 3
- Protein: 0.6
- Sodium: 28.4
- Fiber: 0.1
- Sugar: 0
- Cholesterol: 10.6

30. Green Bean And Potato Soup

Serving: 6 serving(s) | Prep: 20mins | Ready in:

Ingredients

- 12 ounces fresh green beans
- 4 small yukon gold potatoes, peeled and cut into small bite-size chunks
- 6 cups chicken stock (good quality-or vegetable broth)
- 3 tablespoons cider vinegar
- 3 tablespoons honey
- 3 garlic cloves, finely minced
- 1 teaspoon caraway seed
- salt fresh ground pepper, to taste
- 2 tablespoons unsalted butter
- 1 large onion, diced
- 2 celery ribs, diced (with some leaves if possible)
- 2 tablespoons sweet Hungarian paprika (good quality and fresh)
- 3 tablespoons cornstarch
- 3 tablespoons water
- 3/4 cup plain yogurt

Direction

- Cut green beans into 1/4-inch slices crosswise.
- Spray a large soup pot with non-stick cooking spray. Put in green beans, potatoes, stock, vinegar, honey, garlic, caraway, salt and pepper. Bring to a boil, reduce heat to medium-low, cover and simmer until vegetables are tender, about 30 minutes.
- Meanwhile, in a 10-inch skillet, melt the butter over medium heat. Add onion and sauté until softened, about 4 minutes. Add celery and sauté another 3 minutes. Lower heat slightly and sprinkle paprika over mixture. Cook another minute, stirring constantly.
- Scrape onion mixture into green bean pot and add a little water to skillet to deglaze it. Add this to soup pot. Take soup pot off of heat.
- When ready to serve, have soup very hot. Dissolve the cornstarch in the water, making a paste and stir the paste into the yogurt.
- Whisk a ladleful of the hot stock into the yogurt. Turn down heat to low and stir cornstarch mixture into the hot soup. Using a wooden spoon, stir gently until soup has thickened slightly.

- Check for seasoning. Add more salt and pepper if needed, and adjust sweet/sour ratio by adding more vinegar or honey as needed.
- Serve.

Nutrition Information

- Calories: 298.2
- Protein: 10.6
- Total Fat: 8.3
- Saturated Fat: 4
- Sodium: 379.4
- Sugar: 18
- Fiber: 4.7
- Total Carbohydrate: 47.3
- Cholesterol: 21.4

31. Homemade Potato And Cheese Pierogies / Old Fashioned Perogies

Serving: 4 serving(s) | Prep: 20mins | Ready in:

Ingredients

- Potato and Cheese Filling
- 1 tablespoon grated onion
- 2 tablespoons butter
- 2 cups cold mashed potatoes
- 1 cup cottage cheese (or more)
- salt and pepper
- Perogie
- 2 1/2 cups flour
- 1/2 teaspoon salt
- 1 egg
- 2 teaspoons oil
- 3/4 cup warm water

Direction

- Potato and Cheese Filling: Cook the onion in butter until tender.
- Combine it with potatoes and cheese.
- Season to taste with salt and pepper.

- Vary the proportions and ingredients in this recipe to suit your taste.
- Mix the flour with the salt in a deep bowl.
- Add the egg, oil and water to make a medium soft dough.
- Knead on a floured board until the dough is smooth.
- Caution: Too much kneading will toughen the dough.
- Divide the dough into 2 parts.
- Cover and let stand for at least 10 minutes.
- Prepare the filling.
- The filling should be thick enough to hold its shape.
- Roll the dough quite thin on a floured board.
- Cut rounds with a large biscuit cutter, or as most old-world grandmothers did, with the open end of a glass.
- Put the round in the palm of your hand.
- Place a spoonful of filling in it, fold over to form a half circle and press the edges together with the fingers.
- The edges should be free of filling.
- Be sure the edges are sealed well to prevent the filling from running out.
- Place the pierogi on a floured board or tea towel and then cover with another tea towel to prevent them from drying out.
- COOKING: Drop a few pierogies into a large quantity of rapidly boiling salted water.
- Do not attempt to cook too many at a time.
- Stir VERY gently with a wooden spoon to separate them and to prevent them from sticking to the bottom of the pot.
- Continue boiling for 3-4 minutes.
- The cooling period will depend upon the size you made it, the thickness of the dough and the filling.
- Pierogies will be ready when they are puffed.
- Remove them with a perforated spoon or skimmer to a colander and drain thoroughly.
- Place in a deep dish, sprinkle generously with melted butter to prevent them from sticking.
- Cover and keep them hot until all are cooked.
- Serve in a large dish without piling or crowding them.

- Top with melted butter- chopped crisp bacon and/or chopped onions lightly browned in butter.
- REHEATING: One of the great things about perogies, is that they can be made in large quantities, refrigerated, frozen and reheated without loss of quality.
- Many prefer reheated perogies as compared to freshly boiled ones.
- To re-heat, you can: 1) pan fry pierogies in butter or bacon fat until they are light in color or, 2) heat the pierogies in the top of a double boiler or in the oven until they are hot and plump or, 3) deep fry them.

Nutrition Information

- Calories: 512.6
- Saturated Fat: 5.7
- Sodium: 870.3
- Fiber: 3.7
- Cholesterol: 72.8
- Sugar: 3.4
- Total Carbohydrate: 80.2
- Protein: 17.6
- Total Fat: 12.8

32. Hortobagyi Palacsinta Blintz

Serving: 4 serving(s) | Prep: 15mins | Ready in:

Ingredients

- FILLING
- 1 onion, chopped fine
- 1 lb veal, chopped fine
- 1 tablespoon oil
- 1 tablespoon paprika
- 1 cup water
- 2 tablespoons flour
- 1 cup sour cream
- CREPES
- 2 eggs
- 4 cups milk
- 2 teaspoons oil
- salt
- 5 1/2 ounces flour

Direction

- FILLING:
- Fry onion and veal in oil.
- Add paprika.
- Add 1 cup water; cook until tender.
- Remove meat from broth.
- Mix flour in sour cream.
- Add to broth.
- CREPES:
- Add eggs to milk.
- Add oil and salt.
- Mix in flour.
- Drop by tablespoonfuls; swirl to make a thin crepe.
- Add meat filling, to which 4 tablespoons sour cream mixture is added, on top of pancake.
- Make a burrito package.
- Put in pan; repeat until done.
- Pour sauce over.
- Bake for 20 minutes at 425 degrees Fahrenheit until warmed.

Nutrition Information

- Calories: 688
- Total Carbohydrate: 49.4
- Protein: 39.2
- Saturated Fat: 17
- Sugar: 3.6
- Sodium: 298.9
- Fiber: 2.2
- Cholesterol: 250.1
- Total Fat: 36.6

33. Hrutka (Egg Cheese)

Serving: 8 serving(s) | Prep: 10hours | Ready in:

Ingredients

- 1 dozen egg
- 1 quart whole milk, no substitutions
- 1 -2 tablespoon honey
- 1 dash salt
- 1/4 teaspoon vanilla (optional)

Direction

- Beat all ingredients well.
- Pour into a large saucepan and cook very slowly over low heat (stirring often) until it looks kind of like cottage cheese and liquid/curds start to separate.
- Pour the mixture into a round colander or a strainer lined with cheese cloth and form into a ball.
- Hang up over a sink and let drip. Drain for about 3 hours.
- Chill at least 8-10 hours or overnight.
- Can serve cold, room temp or warm.

Nutrition Information

- Calories: 178.2
- Total Fat: 10.5
- Saturated Fat: 4.3
- Protein: 12.2
- Total Carbohydrate: 8.2
- Cholesterol: 291.4
- Sodium: 160.7
- Fiber: 0
- Sugar: 9.1

34. Hungarian Angel Wing Fry Cookies (Csoroge)

Serving: 12 serving(s) | Prep: 0S | Ready in:

Ingredients

- 3 large egg yolks
- 1 tablespoon sour cream
- 1 tablespoon granulated sugar
- 1 tablespoon rum or 1 tablespoon whiskey
- 1 pinch salt
- 1 1/2 cups all-purpose flour, sifted

Direction

- Place in the center of a bread board one cup of flour. Make a dent or well in the center. Add the whole yolks, sour cream, sugar, rum and salt. With a fork mix until the liquids are well combined.
- Gradually work into the flour. The dough should be of the consistency of a noodle dough. Knead for a few minutes to make the dough smooth.
- Split the dough into 2 portions. On a lightly floured board roll out each section until paper thin.
- If you have a pie crimping wheel, use it to cut the dough into squares of 3 1/2-inches or a rectangle of 3 1/2 x 2 1/2-inches. They will have beautiful serrated edges.
- With a paring knife make three or four gashes about 2 to 2 1/2-inches evenly spaced.
- Fry in a deep fat (Lard preferred, Crisco OK) until golden brown.
- Drain on paper towel.
- Sprinkle with sifted confectioners' sugar.

Nutrition Information

- Calories: 79.4
- Total Fat: 1.5
- Saturated Fat: 0.6
- Cholesterol: 52.9
- Sodium: 15.8
- Fiber: 0.4
- Sugar: 1.1
- Total Carbohydrate: 13.2
- Protein: 2.3

35. Hungarian Beef Paprikash

Serving: 4-6 serving(s) | Prep: 20mins | Ready in:

Ingredients

- 1 lb beef tips or 1 lb stew meat, cut into cubes
- salt and pepper
- 2 tablespoons oil, 1 tbsp. butter
- 2 yellow onions, sliced into strings
- 2 garlic cloves, coarsely chopped
- 3 cups red peppers, cut into strips (approx. 4 small peppers)
- 1 (14 ounce) can chopped tomatoes
- 2 tablespoons spicy mustard
- 2 cups beef broth
- 2 tablespoons hot sauce (chili sauce, or tabasco)
- 1 1/2 cups orange juice
- 1 pint sour cream

Direction

- Pat the beef dry, then salt and pepper before placing in the pot.
- Brown the meat on all sides for a few minutes in the pot with oil and butter.
- Transfer beef to a bowl.
- Add onions, garlic and more butter to pot. Sautee until tender, then transfer onion/garlic to a bowl.
- Add can of chopped tomatoes and mustard to pot, stirring and scraping all the bits off bottom of pot.
- Add in the onions and stir until combined with sauce, about 2 minutes.
- Empty the two cups of beef broth into pot, along with the Red Peppers. Stir until slightly softened.
- Add beef, and stir in hot sauce to taste. Remember the hot sauce gains strength as it cooks, so keep testing periodically to get the level heat you want, adding a little at a time.
- Add orange juice and stir over low heat for a few minutes, again testing the level of heat with the hot sauce. Leave uncovered while stirring.
- Once all is to a good boil, cover, reduce heat, and let simmer for one hour. You can even turn it off and let sit for a few hours, to have ready for a meal hours later.

- Now bring the pot to a boil, and add the sour cream. Stir until blended. Sauce should have a rich orange color, and a creamy, not thick texture. If too thick, add more orange juice.
- Update the level "heat" with more hot sauce, if desired.
- Serve over white rice or thick egg noodles. Enjoy!

Nutrition Information

- Calories: 660.7
- Fiber: 4.7
- Sugar: 18
- Total Carbohydrate: 32
- Protein: 30.1
- Total Fat: 47.3
- Saturated Fat: 22.1
- Sodium: 692.4
- Cholesterol: 124.7

36. Hungarian Beef Stew Slow Cooker Style

Serving: 6 serving(s) | Prep: 10mins | Ready in:

Ingredients

- 1 1/4 lbs beef chuck
- 1 lb carrot, sliced
- 2 cups onions, chopped
- 3 cups cabbage, thinly sliced
- 2 cups water
- 1 (6 ounce) can tomato paste
- 1 (8 ounce) package onion and mushroom soup mix
- 1 tablespoon paprika
- 1 teaspoon caraway seed
- 1 cup sour cream
- serve with egg noodles

Direction

- Mix all ingredients except sour cream and noodles in a 3 1/2-quart slow cooker.
- Cook and cover on low 8 hours until tender. Turn off cooker and stir in sour cream until well blended.
- Cook noodles of your choice and serve over.

Nutrition Information

- Calories: 534.5
- Cholesterol: 82.1
- Protein: 24.9
- Total Fat: 30.1
- Fiber: 6.7
- Sugar: 10.9
- Total Carbohydrate: 44.2
- Saturated Fat: 13
- Sodium: 2729.4

37. Hungarian Borscht

Serving: 16 serving(s) | Prep: 30mins | Ready in:

Ingredients

- 10 fluid ounces kraft low calorie catalina salad dressing, no substitutes
- 2 large red beets, peeled and cubed 3/8 inch square
- 2 large carrots, peeled and diced small
- 1 large onion, finely chopped
- 1 small rutabaga, diced small
- 5 cups beef consomme
- 8 cups water
- 19 fluid ounces canned plum tomatoes, including liquid
- 3 large potatoes, peeled and cubed 1/2 inch square
- 3/4 teaspoon caraway seed
- 1 1/2 cups thinly shredded red cabbage
- 1 1/2 cups thinly shredded green cabbage or 1 1/2 cups white cabbage
- 3 large celery ribs, include leaves,chopped small

- 3 cups cauliflower florets
- 1 teaspoon fresh ground black pepper
- 2 tablespoons soy sauce
- 5 teaspoons dried dill weed (or more if desired)
- 1 cup sour cream or 1 cup yogurt

Direction

- In a large frying pan, add Kraft Catalina dressing, beets, carrots, onion, rutabaga and cook on medium-high heat until vegetables are tender, about 15 minutes.
- In a large cooking pot, add beef consommé', water, cooked vegetables, tomatoes including liquid (crush tomatoes before adding to pot), potatoes, caraway seeds, red and green shredded cabbage, celery, cauliflower florets, black pepper and bring to boil.
- Reduce heat and simmer until all vegetables are tender, about 10 minutes.
- Add soy sauce and dill weed and simmer for another 3 minutes.
- Adjust seasonings to taste.
- Serve hot with dollops of sour cream or plain yogurt if desired.

Nutrition Information

- Calories: 124.6
- Total Fat: 3.1
- Fiber: 3.7
- Total Carbohydrate: 20.4
- Protein: 5.3
- Saturated Fat: 1.7
- Sodium: 720
- Sugar: 4.9
- Cholesterol: 7.5

38. Hungarian Cabbage Noodles

Serving: 6 serving(s) | Prep: 10mins | Ready in:

Ingredients

- 5 slices bacon
- 1 1/2 teaspoons salt
- 4 ounces egg noodles (cooked)
- 1/2 cup sour cream
- 1 tablespoon sugar
- 6 cups chopped cabbage
- paprika

Direction

- In a large skillet, cook bacon until crisp.
- Remove from skillet; drain on paper towel and crumble.
- Stir sugar and salt into bacon drippings in skillet.
- Add cabbage; stir till cabbage is coated.
- Cook (covered) over medium heat until cabbage is tender, about 10 or 15 minutes.
- Combine cabbage mixture, noodles and bacon; turn all into a 1 1/2-quart casserole.
- Cover and bake in slow oven (325°) for 45 minutes.
- Uncover; spoon sour cream over top.
- Sprinkle with paprika.
- Return to oven and bake 5 minutes more.

Nutrition Information

- Calories: 225.4
- Sugar: 5
- Total Carbohydrate: 20.5
- Saturated Fat: 5.6
- Sodium: 765.5
- Fiber: 2.2
- Cholesterol: 37.2
- Protein: 6.5
- Total Fat: 13.4

39. Hungarian Cabbage Noodles (Kaposztas Taszta)

Serving: 1 Dish, 4 serving(s) | Prep: 10mins | Ready in:

Ingredients

- 2 tablespoons vegetable oil
- 1/2 large green cabbage, cored and sliced thin
- salt, to taste
- 1 (10 ounce) bag wide egg noodles
- 1 tablespoon unsalted butter
- pepper, to taste

Direction

- Bring 4 quarts of water to a boil in a large pot for the noodles.
- Meanwhile, heat 1 tablespoon of the oil in a large skillet over medium-high heat until shimmering. Add half of the cabbage, season with 1/4 teaspoon of salt, and cook, tossing frequently, until golden brown, 5 - 8 minutes. Transfer the cooked cabbage to a place. Repeat with the remaining cabbage.
- Add 1 tablespoon of salt and the noodles to the boiling water and cook until al dente. Drain the noodles and transfer back to the pot. Add the reserved cabbage and butter, toss to combine, and season to taste with salt and pepper. Serve.

Nutrition Information

- Calories: 396.6
- Saturated Fat: 3.6
- Sodium: 43.4
- Total Fat: 13
- Total Carbohydrate: 59.5
- Cholesterol: 67.5
- Protein: 12.4
- Fiber: 5.9
- Sugar: 6.9

40. Hungarian Cabbage Strudel

Serving: 4 serving(s) | Prep: 30mins | Ready in:

Ingredients

- 8 ounces unsalted butter, more for greasing pan
- 1 lb cabbage, cored and shredded (about 1/2 head)
- 1/2 teaspoon salt
- 1/2 teaspoon fresh ground black pepper
- 10 sheets phyllo dough, defrosted

Direction

- Preheat oven to 350 degrees F; lightly butter a large baking pan and spread cabbage evenly in pan.
- Season with salt and pepper.
- Cut up 4 ounces (1 stick) butter into small pieces, and sprinkle over cabbage; cover with foil, sealing edges.
- Bake until tender and golden, 45 minutes to 60 minutes, occasionally lifting foil and mixing cabbage, then resealing.
- Remove from heat, uncover and allow to cool to room temperature (may be stored, covered and refrigerated, for up to 24 hours; use chilled).
- Set oven temperature to 400 degrees F.
- In a small saucepan, melt remaining 4 ounces butter.
- Place a sheet of parchment paper on a work surface with the narrow end closest to you, and top with a sheet of phyllo dough.
- Brush lengthwise (up and down) with a little butter.
- Top with another sheet of phyllo, and brush again with butter.
- Repeat until all 10 sheets are buttered and stacked.
- Arrange cabbage on dough, at end closest to you, in a thick layer 2 inches deep; spread evenly to edges.
- With the help of the parchment paper, roll phyllo, starting at the end with the cabbage, as you work, adjust parchment paper so that phyllo is rolled, enclosing cabbage, without the paper.
- Brush top of roll with butter, place on baking sheet and bake until golden, about 40 minutes.
- Serve hot or warm.

Nutrition Information

- Calories: 576.5
- Total Fat: 49
- Saturated Fat: 29.9
- Fiber: 3.6
- Cholesterol: 121.9
- Sodium: 546.9
- Sugar: 4.2
- Total Carbohydrate: 31.5
- Protein: 5.5

41. Hungarian Cabbage And Noodles

Serving: 6 serving(s) | Prep: 15mins | Ready in:

Ingredients

- 5 slices bacon
- 1 tablespoon sugar
- 1 1/2 teaspoons salt
- 6 cups chopped cabbage
- 4 ounces medium noodles, cooked
- 1/2 cup sour cream
- paprika

Direction

- In a large skillet, cook bacon till crisp.
- Remove from skillet; drain and crumble.
- Stir sugar and salt into bacon drippings in skillet.
- Add cabbage; stir till cabbage is coated.
- Cook, covered, over medium heat till cabbage is tender about 10 minutes.
- Combine cabbage mixture, noodles, and bacon; put into 1 1/2-quart casserole.
- Cover and bake in a 325-degree oven for 45 minutes.
- Uncover; spoon sour cream over top.
- Sprinkle with paprika.
- Return to oven and bake for 5 minutes more.

Nutrition Information

- Calories: 178.5
- Fiber: 1.8
- Saturated Fat: 5.4
- Sugar: 4.7
- Total Carbohydrate: 11.7
- Cholesterol: 26.8
- Protein: 4.7
- Total Fat: 13
- Sodium: 762.4

42. Hungarian Cabbage And Potatoes

Serving: 6-8 serving(s) | Prep: 10mins | Ready in:

Ingredients

- 1 head cabbage, shredded
- 6 medium potatoes, peeled and diced
- 3 tablespoons oil
- 4 tablespoons flour
- 1 garlic clove, minced
- 1/2 teaspoon caraway seed
- 1 teaspoon Hungarian paprika
- salt
- pepper

Direction

- Boil potatoes until half done.
- Add cabbage and more water if necessary, to barely cover. Continue to cook gently until cabbage is cooked but still crisp. Stir cabbage and potato now and then.
- While cabbage and potato are cooking melt oil in saucepan and add flour. Cook over low heat stirring constantly until mixture is light tan in color.
- Remove from heat; add garlic caraway seed and paprika; mix to combine. When cabbage

and potato are cooked add flour mixture to pot and stir in quickly so lumps do not form.
- Continue to simmer so flavors blend about 10-minute Season w/ salt and pepper to taste.

Nutrition Information

- Calories: 281.7
- Protein: 7.1
- Fiber: 8.5
- Sugar: 7.1
- Total Carbohydrate: 50.1
- Cholesterol: 0
- Total Fat: 7.3
- Saturated Fat: 1
- Sodium: 40.4

43. Hungarian Cauliflower Soup

Serving: 4 serving(s) | Prep: 10mins | Ready in:

Ingredients

- 1 large cauliflower
- 4 tablespoons butter
- 1 tablespoon flour
- 1/4 teaspoon paprika
- 1 teaspoon salt (may need more)
- 2 tablespoons parsley, chopped
- 1 cup sour cream
- 1 chicken bouillon cube (optional)
- Dumplings
- 3 eggs
- 2 tablespoons sour cream
- 1 cup flour, may need more

Direction

- Break cauliflower into sections removing tough fibers.
- Add enough water to cover. Cook until tender. (I used frozen.).(Mash up when cooked).

- I added chicken bouillon cube and 1 teaspoon dried parsley; if using the fresh parsley, put it in with the dumplings.
- (I would add the dumplings here before the roux).
- Make roux with butter, flour, paprika, and salt. (Add when noodles are floating).
- Add to soup gradually, stirring frequently.
- Add sour cream right before you add dumplings. (Or just sour cream).
- Make dumplings: Blend eggs, sour cream, and flour together; do not beat. Drop by 1/2 teaspoons into soup for last 10 minutes cooking. Cover. Cook on very low heat.

Nutrition Information

- Calories: 452.4
- Protein: 13.7
- Total Carbohydrate: 38.1
- Cholesterol: 203.1
- Total Fat: 28.6
- Saturated Fat: 16
- Sodium: 851.6
- Fiber: 5.2
- Sugar: 6.5

44. Hungarian Cheese Spread (Liptauer)

Serving: 12 Tblsp, 12 serving(s) | Prep: 10mins | Ready in:

Ingredients

- 8 ounces cream cheese
- 1 cup cottage cheese
- 3 tablespoons capers
- 1 teaspoon caraway seed
- 1/2 teaspoon dry mustard
- 2 teaspoons paprika

Direction

- Cream together all ingredients.
- Place into a bowl or pretty mold covered with plastic wrap. Cover top of cheese with plastic wrap.
- Refrigerate for at least 2 hours overnight is best.
- Unmold on to a serving plate and surround with rye bread squares, fresh veggies, or crackers.

Nutrition Information

- Calories: 86.7
- Protein: 3.8
- Saturated Fat: 4.7
- Fiber: 0.3
- Sugar: 0.1
- Total Carbohydrate: 1.4
- Cholesterol: 23.4
- Total Fat: 7.5
- Sodium: 190.7

45. Hungarian Cheese Filled Coffee Cake

Serving: 24 serving(s) | Prep: 30mins | Ready in:

Ingredients

- 2 (1/4 ounce) packages yeast
- 1/2 cup warm water
- 1 cup butter
- 5 cups flour
- 1 1/4 cups sugar
- 1/2 teaspoon salt
- 6 egg yolks
- 1 cup sour cream
- 1 (8 ounce) package cream cheese
- 2 whole eggs
- 1 teaspoon vanilla
- 1 (10 ounce) jar apricot jam
- powdered sugar

Direction

- Dissolve yeast in the warm water. Melt butter.
- Sift flour with 3/4 C of the sugar and the salt into a large bowl.
- Beat egg yolks until thick and light; blend in the sour cream and melted butter; stir in the dissolved yeast.
- Gradually stir the egg yolk mixture into the dry ingredients, mixing to make a soft, smooth dough. Turn out on a lightly floured board and knead for 5 minutes, or until the dough is smooth. Turn into a bowl, cover, and let rise until almost doubled in bulk.
- Prepare cheese filling. Cream the cheese until light and blend in the remaining 1/2 C sugar. Add the whole eggs, one at a time, and beat until smooth. Blend in vanilla.
- Punch down dough and knead a few minutes. Lightly flour a board; roll out dough into a large circle, about 18 inches in diameter, and lay it over a greased 3-quart ring mold (you may use two 9" ring molds. Roll 1/2 dough 13" thick for each 9" ring mold). Fit the dough down into the bottom and the sides of the ring mold, being careful not to poke holes in it, and let it hang over the outside. Pour in the cheese filling (1/2 cheese fill for each 9" ring mold).
- Lift outside edges of the dough, and lap it over the filling, sealing to the inside ring of dough. Cut a cross in the dough which covers the center of the ring mold and fold each triangle formed back over the ring, completely encasing the filling.
- Let rise until doubled in bulk or until the dough comes to the top of the pan.
- Bake in a moderate oven (350 degrees) for 40 minutes, or until golden brown and a toothpick inserted comes out clean. (For 9" ring mold, bake for 30 minutes.) Let cool for 10 minutes, then turn out with top side down onto a rack.
- When bread ring is cool, heat jam until it runs easily; carefully spoon jam over the ring. When set, dust lightly with powdered sugar by shaking about 2 tbsp sugar through a sieve. To serve, slice the ring in 1" wedges.

Nutrition Information

- Calories: 303.3
- Saturated Fat: 8.3
- Sodium: 167.6
- Sugar: 16.3
- Protein: 5
- Total Fat: 14.5
- Fiber: 0.9
- Total Carbohydrate: 39
- Cholesterol: 92.7

46. Hungarian Chicken Breasts

Serving: 4 serving(s) | Prep: 5mins | Ready in:

Ingredients

- 4 boneless skinless chicken breast halves (from two whole chicken breasts)
- 1 tablespoon butter
- 1 tablespoon vegetable oil
- 1 red sweet bell pepper, cut into 1-inch squares
- 1 yellow sweet bell pepper, cut into 1-inch squares
- 1 tablespoon tarragon vinegar
- 3/4 cup whipping cream
- salt and pepper, to taste
- 1/2 cup snipped fresh chives

Direction

- Heat butter and oil in heavy skillet. Add peppers. Sauté over medium heat until tender-crisp - about 3-4 minutes - stirring occasionally. Remove from pan.
- Add chicken breasts to skillet. Sauté for 10-15 minutes until just cooked through, turning once. Remove from the pan and keep warm.
- Add the vinegar to the pan. Bring to a boil, scraping up browned bits. Add the cream and boil until reduced by about half.
- Add chicken to the pan. Sprinkle with salt and pepper. Simmer until chicken is heated, basting with the sauce.

- Serve chicken with sauce spooned over. Garnish with sautéed peppers. Sprinkle with the snipped fresh chives.

Nutrition Information

- Calories: 367.6
- Sodium: 181.5
- Fiber: 1.2
- Total Carbohydrate: 6.2
- Cholesterol: 144.3
- Total Fat: 26.1
- Saturated Fat: 13.2
- Sugar: 1.4
- Protein: 26.9

47. Hungarian Chicken For The Pressure Cooker

Serving: 4-5 serving(s) | Prep: 20mins | Ready in:

Ingredients

- 1 tablespoon vegetable oil
- 3 chicken drumsticks, bone in and skinned
- 3 chicken thighs, bone-in and skinned
- 1 medium onion, coarsely chopped
- 2 teaspoons paprika
- 1 cup boiling water
- 2 chicken bouillon cubes
- 1 medium tomatoes, peeled and coarsely chopped
- 1 teaspoon salt
- 1/2 cup sour cream
- 1/2 cup water
- 1/3 cup cornstarch

Direction

- Heat the oil in the pressure cooker over medium-high heat until hot. Add the chicken pieces and cook until golden-brown on all sides. Transfer chicken to a plate.
- Mix the 1 cup water and 2 c cubes, until dissolved.
- Add the onion, paprika, and bouillon and stir to mix. Add the chicken pieces back to the pot and add the tomato on top, but don't stir it inches Add the salt.
- Lock on the lid and bring to pressure over high heat. Reduce heat to medium and cook for about 7 minutes. Remove from heat and let sit for 5 minutes to finish cooking.
- Gently release any remaining pressure and transfer the chicken to a plate.
- Whisk the sour cream in a small bowl until smooth. Add 1/4 cup of the liquid from the pot and whisk until smooth.
- Put the pot back on a burner over medium heat, until sauce is lightly bubbling. Pour the sour cream mixture into the pot and whisk to mix.
- Whisk together the 1/2 cup of water and cornstarch. Slowly add this to the pot and whisk it in until the sauce is not quite as thick as gravy. You may not use all the water/cornstarch mixture. Add the chicken pieces back to the pot.
- Serve over seasoned rice or egg noodles.

Nutrition Information

- Calories: 394.5
- Total Fat: 25.4
- Total Carbohydrate: 15.9
- Saturated Fat: 8.7
- Sodium: 1072.8
- Fiber: 1.2
- Sugar: 2.5
- Cholesterol: 116.5
- Protein: 24.7

48. Hungarian Chocolate Cream Bars

Serving: 25-30 serving(s) | Prep: 50mins | Ready in:

Ingredients

- CAKE
- 4 large eggs, separated
- 1⁄4 teaspoon cream of tartar
- 2⁄3 cup sugar, divided
- 3⁄4 cup sweet butter, room temp
- 9 tablespoons cocoa powder
- 1⁄2 cup all-purpose flour, sifted
- FILLING
- 2 cups heavy cream
- 12 ounces semi-sweet chocolate chips
- 1 tablespoon instant coffee, powdered
- 1⁄8 cup rum (optional)
- GLAZE
- 5 ounces semisweet chocolate
- 1 ounce unsweetened chocolate
- 4 tablespoons sweet butter
- 1 teaspoon vegetable oil
- 1 tablespoon Karo syrup

Direction

- TO MAKE CAKE: Preheat oven to 350°F; grease a 9 x 13-inch pan. Line pan with wax paper and grease the wax paper.
- Beat the egg whites lightly, add cream of tartar and beat at a high speed.
- When shiny, gradually add 1/3 cup of sugar, continuing to beat until stiff.
- In a separate mixing bowl, place the egg yolks, remaining sugar and butter and beat until light and fluffy. Add the cocoa and mix thoroughly. Add a large dollop of egg whites to chocolate mixture and whip until blended.
- Then pour the rest of the egg whites over the chocolate mixture and sprinkle the flour over the egg whites. Fold gently with a spatula until the egg whites and flour are incorporated.
- Immediately spread the batter in the prepared pan. Smooth out to edges and corners. Bake 10-15 minutes at 350°F until cake is done. Run a knife around edges and invert cake on a wire rack to cool.
- TO MAKE FILLING: in a saucepan, combine cream, chocolate chips and instant coffee.

- Cook over low heat until mixture is smooth and slightly thickened.
- Cover saucepan and refrigerate until very cold.
- When chilled, add rum (if using) and whip in a chilled bowl at medium speed until firm. Be careful not to over beat or the filling may separate.
- TO MAKE GLAZE (do NOT make this until ALL OTHER steps are completed): in a small saucepan, melt all ingredients over a low flame. Mix until very smooth.
- Cool for 15 minutes and mix again. Use immediately, as the sauce thickens as it cools.
- TO ASSEMBLE: cut cake horizontally into halves. Lightly sprinkle bottom half with rum. Spread filling over bottom layer.
- Place top layer on bottom half and spread filling over top.
- Refrigerate or freeze until very firm.
- When very cold, set the cake on a wire rack. Pour the warm glaze over the cake. Refrigerate again until firm. Cut with a sharp knife, wiping the blade after each cut.
- You can freeze cut squares.

Nutrition Information

- Calories: 280.4
- Total Fat: 23.3
- Sodium: 23.1
- Total Carbohydrate: 20.2
- Protein: 3.6
- Saturated Fat: 14.1
- Fiber: 2.6
- Sugar: 13.1
- Cholesterol: 79.5

49. Hungarian Cookies

Serving: 36 cookies | Prep: 30mins | Ready in:

Ingredients

- 1 cup butter (margarine will not do)
- 1 cup granulated sugar
- 2 egg yolks
- 2 cups flour
- 1/2 cup chopped walnuts
- 1/2 cup seedless red raspberry jam

Direction

- Preheat the oven to 325.
- Grease the bottom and sides of a 9x9x2 cake pan and set aside.
- Cream the butter, sugar, and yolks.
- Fold in flour and walnuts.
- Divide the batter in half. Do not over handle the dough. One half will serve as the top layer and the other as the bottom.
- Take a piece of batter and gently flatten it using your fingers. You will see that the batter tends to make its own sections. Work with those. Place this section on the bottom of the cake pan and continue until you have covered the bottom of the cake pan in a patchwork manner. Do not worry about the dough not looking smooth in the pan, you will fix that in a minute.
- If you have leftover dough from the half, fill in holes and build up areas that may be thinner than others.
- Take the back of a spoon and gently smooth the edges of the dough together so no holes are apparent.
- Spread a thin layer of jam over the dough. Do not make the layer thick, you are not making PB and J here.
- Use the final half of batter to make the top layer using the same technique as above.
- Place in the oven at 325 degrees for 30-45 minutes. At around 25 minutes start peaking in the oven, the dough should be a nice golden-brown color when it is finished.
- Let cookies cool completely before cutting into small squares.

Nutrition Information

- Calories: 117.7
- Protein: 1.2
- Total Fat: 6.5
- Sodium: 38.3
- Fiber: 0.3
- Total Carbohydrate: 14.2
- Cholesterol: 24.1
- Saturated Fat: 3.4
- Sugar: 7.8

50. Hungarian Cookies For Beginners

Serving: 26 serving(s) | Prep: 30mins | Ready in:

Ingredients

- 4 cups unsifted flour
- 3 teaspoons baking powder
- 1/2 cup sugar
- 1 lb margarine
- 3 eggs
- 2 teaspoons vanilla
- 2 teaspoons milk
- 1 beaten egg
- 1/2 cup jam

Direction

- Sift together dry ingredients.
- Cut in margarine as for pie crust.
- Add eggs, vanilla and milk, just enough to hold dough together. Do not work this dough, just blend ingredients.
- Roll out and cut into squares 3x3 inch, not too thin.
- Fill with any desired filling.
- Brush top with beaten egg.
- Bake at 350 degrees Fahrenheit until golden brown.

Nutrition Information

- Calories: 240.3
- Total Fat: 15

- Sodium: 219.9
- Sugar: 7
- Total Carbohydrate: 23.2
- Cholesterol: 32.6
- Protein: 3.1
- Saturated Fat: 2.7
- Fiber: 0.6

51. Hungarian Cream Cheese Spread

Serving: 4-6 serving(s) | Prep: 5mins | Ready in:

Ingredients

- 8 ounces cream cheese
- 1 tablespoon Hungarian paprika
- 1/2 green pepper (thinly sliced)
- salt

Direction

- Mix cream cheese and paprika.
- (It should become salmon colored).
- Salt to taste.
- Spread generously over bread.
- Garnish with thin green pepper slices.
- YUM! EAT IT ALL UP!

Nutrition Information

- Calories: 205.8
- Total Fat: 20
- Saturated Fat: 12.5
- Sodium: 168.9
- Fiber: 0.9
- Sugar: 0.7
- Total Carbohydrate: 3.2
- Cholesterol: 62.4
- Protein: 4.7

52. Hungarian Cucumber Salad With Sour Cream Dressing

Serving: 4 serving(s) | Prep: 10mins | Ready in:

Ingredients

- 4 cucumbers
- 1 clove garlic
- 1 teaspoon sugar
- 1/4 teaspoon salt
- 1/4 cup vinegar
- 3/4 cup sour cream

Direction

- Peel cukes.
- Drag fork tines down length of peeled cucumbers to create long groves that will look very nice when you slice cucumbers very, very thin.
- Put in mixing bowl.
- Peel and chop clove of garlic.
- Add salt and sugar slices.
- Mix in sour cream.
- Add vinegar and toss well, I use my hands, till cucumbers slices and sour cream are all frothy and foamy.
- Place in serving dish and sprinkle a little paprika on top for decoration, and serve well chilled.

Nutrition Information

- Calories: 136.2
- Total Fat: 8.8
- Saturated Fat: 5.1
- Sodium: 186.3
- Total Carbohydrate: 13.5
- Cholesterol: 22.4
- Protein: 2.9
- Fiber: 1.5
- Sugar: 7.6

53. Hungarian Deep Fried Angel Wing Cookies (Csoroge)

Serving: 30 cookies | Prep: 15mins | Ready in:

Ingredients

- oil (lard tastes the best, but it's not the healthiest and oil and shortening taste fine) or lard (lard tastes the best, but it's not the healthiest and oil and shortening taste fine) or shortening, for deep frying (lard tastes the best, but it's not the healthiest and oil and shortening taste fine)
- 2 cups flour, sifted
- 1 tablespoon sugar
- 1/2 teaspoon salt
- 3 egg yolks, slightly beaten
- 1/2 cup thick sour cream
- 2 1/2 teaspoons whiskey or 2 1/2 teaspoons dark rum
- 1/2 teaspoon vanilla extract
- 2 -3 tablespoons powdered sugar or 2 -3 tablespoons vanilla powdered sugar, to dust cookies

Direction

- About 20 minutes before frying fill a deep saucepan halfway to 2/3 full of oil, lard, or shortening, and heat slowly to 365°F or follow the manufacturer's directions for set-up if using an automatic deep-fryer.
- Sift together flour, sugar, and salt into a bowl.
- Mix together the egg yolks, sour cream, whiskey, and vanilla, then make a well in the center of the dry mixture and pour the wet mixture inches.
- Mix the ingredients until all of the flour is moistened.
- Let dough rest 1-2 minutes.
- Turn dough out onto a lightly floured surface and knead by folding opposite side over towards you, then using the heels of your hands to push the dough away, then give it a quarter turn and repeat process just until ingredients are well blended (always turn the dough in the same direction and use as little additional flour as possible).
- Shape dough into a smooth ball and roll out on a lightly floured surface into a rectangle 1/8-inch thick (if you don't have enough space to do this, divide dough in half first, then roll out the halves separately).
- Use a spatula to loosen the dough, lift it slightly and sprinkle a little flour underneath anywhere the dough sticks.
- With a floured knife cut the dough into diamond shapes about 2-inches wide at the center and 6-inches long (you can make a cardboard pattern beforehand and use that as a guide if you wish).
- Make a 1-inch slit lengthwise at the center of each cookie, and pull one end through the opening, twisting slightly as you do.
- Deep fry only one layer of cookies at a time (don't crowd the pan).
- With a fork, turn the cookies several times as they fry and as they rise to the surface, but be careful not to pierce the cookie.
- Fry until lightly browned (about 3 minutes).
- Drain cookies over fat for a few seconds and then drain on paper towels.
- Sprinkle cookies with powdered sugar while still hot.

Nutrition Information

- Calories: 48.3
- Fiber: 0.2
- Total Fat: 1.3
- Sodium: 41.7
- Sugar: 1
- Total Carbohydrate: 7.5
- Cholesterol: 20.6
- Protein: 1.2
- Saturated Fat: 0.7

54. Hungarian Dumplings

Serving: 4 serving(s) | Prep: 10mins | Ready in:

Ingredients

- 2 eggs
- 2 tablespoons freshly rendered lard or 2 tablespoons oil
- 1/2 cup water
- 1/2 cup milk
- 2 1/2 cups all-purpose flour
- 2 1/2 teaspoons salt
- 1/4 teaspoon baking powder
- 4 quarts water

Direction

- Using an electric mixer, blend the eggs, lard or oil, water, and milk.
- Stir the flour together with 1/2 t of the salt and the baking powder in a dry bowl.
- Blend this mixture into the liquid. Mix well and set aside for a moment.
- Bring 4 quarts of water to a boil and add 2 teaspoons of salt.
- Using a Spaetzle maker or Spaetzle press, squeeze the dough into the boiling water. Use about 1/3 of the dough for each batch. When the dumplings float to the surface, they are done.
- Remove them with a slotted spoon and place in a colander. They can be served this way with Paprika Gravy or pan-fried with a little butter, just until they are a bit golden, and topped with parsley.
- NOTE: These dumplings can also be made by using a piping bag or dropping very small amounts from a spoon. The latter takes much longer.

Nutrition Information

- Calories: 398.5
- Saturated Fat: 4.1
- Fiber: 2.1
- Total Carbohydrate: 61.3
- Cholesterol: 116.1
- Protein: 12.2
- Total Fat: 10.8
- Sodium: 1547.2
- Sugar: 0.4

55. Hungarian Dumplings Again

Serving: 6 serving(s) | Prep: 30mins | Ready in:

Ingredients

- 3 cups flour, sifted
- 7 eggs, beaten
- 3/4 cup milk or 3/4 cup water
- 1 teaspoon salt
- 3 ounces butter, melted

Direction

- Mix flour, eggs, milk or water and salt together.
- Scrape bits from a plate into boiling water, or use a dumpling maker.
- Cook 15 minutes; rinse with cold water and drain.
- Add melted butter.

Nutrition Information

- Calories: 434.4
- Saturated Fat: 9.9
- Sodium: 567.1
- Fiber: 1.7
- Total Carbohydrate: 49.6
- Cholesterol: 281.5
- Protein: 14.9
- Total Fat: 19
- Sugar: 0.6

56. Hungarian Egg And Potato Casserole

Serving: 6-8 serving(s) | Prep: 45mins | Ready in:

Ingredients

- 6 potatoes
- 8 eggs
- 1 onion, chopped
- 1 tablespoon oil
- 1/2 teaspoon salt
- 1/4 teaspoon pepper
- 1/2 cup margarine
- 1 cup sour cream
- 1 cup gruyere cheese, shredded
- 2 tablespoons dry breadcrumbs
- 2 tablespoons Hungarian paprika

Direction

- Preheat oven to 350°F (175°C).
- Bring a large pot of salted water to a boil. Add unpeeled potatoes and cook until tender but still firm - about 15 minutes. Drain, cool, peel and cut in 1/4-inch slices.
- Place eggs in a saucepan and cover with cold water. Bring water to a boil and immediately remove from heat. Cover and let stand in hot water for about 15 minutes. Remove from water, cool, peel and slice.
- In another saucepan sauté onion in oil until translucent and add margarine, sour cream, salt and pepper.
- In a casserole dish layer potatoes and eggs, pouring a small amount of the sauce on each layer. Ensure that the first and last layers are potatoes.
- Sprinkle cheese on top of the casserole followed by breadcrumbs and paprika.
- Bake in preheated oven for 30 minutes.

Nutrition Information

- Calories: 444
- Sodium: 398.9
- Fiber: 5.8
- Sugar: 4.4
- Total Fat: 22.5
- Saturated Fat: 10.3
- Total Carbohydrate: 42.3
- Cholesterol: 287.7
- Protein: 19.4

57. Hungarian Gala Palacsinta Cake

Serving: 8 serving(s) | Prep: 35mins | Ready in:

Ingredients

- palacsinta batter
- 3 cups sifted all-purpose flour
- 1 tablespoon sugar, added to flour
- 1 1/2 teaspoons salt
- 6 eggs
- 1 1/2 cups milk
- 6 tablespoons melted butter
- 1 1/2 cups soda water (about)
- 3 tablespoons cooking oil
- filling 1
- 2 ounces semisweet chocolate, grated
- 1 cup coarsely chopped walnuts (4 ounces)
- 1/2 cup sifted vanilla confectioners' sugar
- filling 2
- 1/2 cup apricot jam
- 1 -2 tablespoon brandy or 1 -2 tablespoon water
- filling 3
- 1 cup pot cheese or 1 cup small curd cottage cheese
- 1 egg, separated
- 4 tablespoons sifted vanilla confectioners' sugar
- 1 teaspoon grated fresh lemon rind
- 2 tablespoons golden seedless raisins
- topping
- 3 egg whites
- 1/2 cup vanilla sugar

Direction

- FOR THE BATTER: Mix the flour and salt and one tablespoon sugar together in a big bowl.
- Work in the eggs, one at a time, then very gradually add the milk, beating well as you go along.
- Beat in the melted butter and strain the batter to remove any large lumps.
- Cover and refrigerate for at least 2 hours or overnight.
- Just before using, shake or stir the batter and pour in as much soda water as needed to make a thin batter, the consistency of light cream.
- Make each palacsinta separately: heat a 6 1/2-inch crepe pan or a small frying pan with sloping sides until very hot, then brush with cooking oil.
- When it starts to smoke, remove from the heat and pour 2 to 3 tablespoons of batter into the pan (work with a ladle the right size, if possible).
- Quickly turn the pan around so the batter flows to the sides, thinly coating the entire bottom.
- A palacsinta is supposed to be very thin, as thin as it can be without getting lacy.
- Pour any excess batter back into the bowl.
- Put the pan back on the heat for about a minute, then give it a couple of good jerks to loosen the palacsinta, then flip it if you can or turn it over by hand, using a spatula to lift it up out of the pan first.
- Cook briefly on the second side and slide it into a warm dish or pie plate.
- Continue making palacsinta until you have at least three per person.
- Keep the palacsinta warm on the back of the stove or in the warming oven, or make them several hours in advance and warm them up later.
- The palacsinta batter may also be made in a blender: put the milk, eggs, salt, flour and melted butter in the jar, in that order.
- Blend at top speed for about 1 minute, then scrape down the sides of the jar and blend another few seconds.
- Cover and refrigerate for 2 hours or overnight; just before making the palacsinta, shake or stir the batter and ADD the SODA water.
- Make the palacsinta and set them aside while preparing the fillings in separate dishes.
- Filling 1: Mix the grated chocolate with the chopped walnuts and confectioners' sugar.
- Set it aside.
- Filling 2: Thin the jam with brandy or water, and mash up any large pieces of fruit.
- Put that to one side.
- Filling 3: Strain the pot cheese and force it through a potato ricer.
- Mix it well with the egg yolk, confectioners' sugar, and lemon rind, and stir in the raisins.
- Beat the egg white until stiff, then fold it into the pot cheese mixture.
- To form the rakott palacsinta, lightly butter an 8-inch springform pan and place a palacsinta on the bottom.
- Spread it with some nut and chocolate filling (number 1), and cover with a second palacsinta.
- Spread that with a thin layer of apricot jam (number 2), and cover it with another palacsinta.
- Spread it with the pot cheese filling (number 3), and cover with a fourth palacsinta.
- REPEAT and continue the layering process until you reach the top of the pan; end with a palacsinta.
- Three quarters of an hour before serving, preheat the oven to 300 F and beat the egg whites with the sugar until stiff and shiny.
- Pile the meringue on the top palacsinta and place the pan in the oven to bake for 30 minutes or more, or until the meringue is lightly browned ("pink").
- Remove the sides of the pan and transfer the rakott palacsinta to a platter.
- Serve hot, cut in wedges like a cake.
- The Hungarian Cookbook.
- Susan Derecskey.

Nutrition Information

- Calories: 627.7
- Total Fat: 33.5
- Saturated Fat: 11.8
- Cholesterol: 214.4
- Sodium: 622
- Fiber: 3.5
- Sugar: 21.2
- Total Carbohydrate: 68.4
- Protein: 16.6

58. Hungarian Goulash (Gulyas) Soup

Serving: 4-6 serving(s) | Prep: 20mins | Ready in:

Ingredients

- 1 kg beef, diced (shank, shin or shoulder)
- 2 middle size red onions, chopped
- 3 pieces carrots, sliced
- 1 -2 piece turnip, sliced
- 1 piece bell pepper, sliced
- 1 piece tomatoes, sliced
- 4 -5 pieces potatoes, diced
- 1 tablespoon ground paprika
- 1 pinch cumin
- 1/2 teaspoon ground pepper
- 1/2 teaspoon chili powder
- 3 1/2 cups water (or as much soup or stew you want)
- 1 vegetable stock cube (optional)
- Egg noodles
- 1 egg
- 1 pinch salt
- 150 g flour (or till becomes hard paste)
- 1 teaspoon water

Direction

- Fry the chopped onions on cooking oil till they glaze. Take it off from hob and add grounded paprika. (If you leave it on the fire and add paprika it will make it bitter).

- Add diced meat. Now you can put it on the fire again. Stir well paprika, onion and meat.
- Add water and steam with lid on till the meat is half cooked. Keep adding enough water. Stir it every few minutes so it won't burn.
- Add as much cold water as much soup you want. Boil it. Salt it.
- When boiled add all the vegetables and cook till everything is softened. It takes a while, especially for the meat.
- Near the end add the spices (cumin, cube, chili, pepper) and salt again if needed.
- Add egg noodles.
- Egg noodles: mix egg and flour and teaspoon water together till it's hard enough. Pick pea-sized bits off it and put it in the soup towards the end and cook it till they come up to the surface. Then they ready.

Nutrition Information

- Calories: 1869.3
- Fiber: 2.8
- Sugar: 2.8
- Total Fat: 179.2
- Saturated Fat: 74.2
- Sodium: 139.2
- Total Carbohydrate: 35.4
- Cholesterol: 294
- Protein: 26.9

59. Hungarian Goulash (With Dumplings)

Serving: 6-8 serving(s) | Prep: 30mins | Ready in:

Ingredients

- Goulash
- 2 tablespoons oil
- 2 onions, chopped
- 2 garlic cloves, chopped
- 2 (8 ounce) packages stewing beef
- 1 (800 ml) can chopped tomatoes

- 2 tablespoons paprika
- 10 cups water
- 6 beef bouillon cubes
- salt and pepper, to taste
- 2 bell peppers, chopped
- 2 large potatoes, cubed
- Dumplings
- 1 cup flour
- 1/2 teaspoon baking powder
- 1/4 teaspoon salt
- 1/2 cup milk

Direction

- Warm the oil in the stock pot over medium heat.
- Add the onions and the garlic, stirring for about five minutes.
- Add the beef, and cook until mostly brown (it'll continue to cook in the stew).
- When the meat is mostly brown, add the can of tomatoes, the paprika, the water, and cubes of beef bouillon (I suggest crumbling it before hand).
- Cover and increase heat until it boils.
- When it boils, decrease heat to a simmer, cover, and let simmer for 1.5-2 hours.
- Add the bell peppers and potatoes.
- Let the stew continue to simmer for 20 minutes.
- In the meantime, mix the flour, baking powder and salt in a mixing bowl.
- Add the milk, and stir thoroughly.
- Flour your hands and roll the dough into half-inch balls. It will be sticky!
- Drop the balls into the simmering stew, and wait until they rise to the surface.
- Enjoy!

Nutrition Information

- Calories: 473.4
- Sodium: 815.1
- Total Carbohydrate: 50.4
- Protein: 21.8
- Total Fat: 21.2

- Sugar: 7
- Cholesterol: 54.2
- Saturated Fat: 7.4
- Fiber: 6.6

60. Hungarian Goulash My Way

Serving: 6 serving(s) | Prep: 30mins | Ready in:

Ingredients

- 2 lbs boneless chuck roast, cut into 1-inch chunks
- kosher salt
- ground pepper
- 2 tablespoons all-purpose flour
- 1 tablespoon olive oil
- 4 medium sweet onions, sliced and separated into rings
- 8 ounces portabella mushrooms or 8 ounces cremini mushrooms, cleaned and cut in half
- 1 head garlic, peeled or 12 garlic cloves
- 1/2 cup sweet red wine
- 1 3/4 cups beef broth
- 1 (4 ounce) jardiced roasted red peppers
- 1/4 cup sweet Hungarian paprika
- 4 cups noodles, cooked and buttered
- 1 cup low-fat sour cream

Direction

- Place beef chunks in a large bowl. Sprinkle liberally with kosher salt and freshly ground pepper. Toss with the flour.
- Heat a heavy Dutch oven over medium high heat and add the olive oil. Swirl to coat the bottom of the pan. Place beef chunks in a single layer and brown on two sides. You will probably need to do this in batches. Do not crowd the meat or it will boil instead of brown. Remove browned beef chunks to a bowl.
- Reduce heat to medium-low. To the drippings in the Dutch oven, add the sweet onion rings, mushrooms, and garlic. Toss to coat with the

olive oil. Cover tightly and sweat the vegetables, stirring occasionally, until the onions are limp but not browned and mushrooms are releasing their liquid, about 10 minutes.

- Add red wine to the vegetables and cook 2 minutes, scraping up browned bits from the bottom. Add beef broth, roasted red peppers, and paprika. Return beef and any accumulated juices to the pan. Stir until well-combined. Cover tightly, reduce heat and simmer on low heat for 1 1/2 to 2 hours, stirring occasionally, until beef is fork tender.
- Remove Dutch oven from heat and wait for boiling to subside. Taste and add additional salt if necessary.
- Serve goulash over hot buttered noodles with a dollop of sour cream.

Nutrition Information

- Calories: 482.9
- Protein: 40.8
- Total Fat: 18.5
- Sugar: 5.3
- Total Carbohydrate: 37.5
- Fiber: 4.7
- Cholesterol: 136.8
- Saturated Fat: 8
- Sodium: 675.5

61. Hungarian Goulash With Red Wine

Serving: 6 serving(s) | Prep: 10mins | Ready in:

Ingredients

- 2 -3 lbs stewing beef, cut into cubes
- 1/2 cup bacon, cut into small pieces
- 1/2 teaspoon salt
- 1/4 teaspoon black pepper
- 2 tablespoons sweet Hungarian paprika
- 1 tablespoon caraway seed (less if you like)

- 1 bay leaf
- 1 -2 green peppers or 1 -2 red pepper, in 1 inch pieces
- 1 1/2 cups beef stock (or water with stock cubes see stock cubes info on package)
- 1 1/2 cups of a dry red wine (the more flavour the better, if I don't have wine I increase the stock amount and add a bit of vineg)
- 3 -4 cloves garlic, minced or in cut in small pieces
- 1 big onion, cut small
- some sour cream, if you like it creamier (optional)
- 1/2 teaspoon hot paprika, if you like it hot (optional)

Direction

- Fry bacon pieces in a deep pan for some minutes until the fat comes out.
- Brown beef in bacon fat with the bacon, stirring.
- Add onion and garlic cloves and brown, stirring.
- Add pepper pieces and paprika and stir.
- Add all other ingredients and cook covered on low heat for 1 1/2-2 hours or until tender Add more water if needed or if it is too thin take the cover off and evaporate the surplus water.
- Take out bay leaf and add sour cream if you prefer it.
- Serve with buttered noodles or with some bread dumplings.

Nutrition Information

- Calories: 329.3
- Total Fat: 12.8
- Sodium: 643.9
- Fiber: 2
- Cholesterol: 104.9
- Protein: 36.1
- Saturated Fat: 4.9
- Sugar: 2.2
- Total Carbohydrate: 7.5

62. Hungarian Goulash With Sauerkraut

Serving: 6 serving(s) | Prep: 15mins | Ready in:

Ingredients

- 1 tablespoon lite olive oil
- 1 lb beef, stewing meat in 1-inch cubes
- 1 lb pork, cut into 1 "cubes
- 2 medium onions, sliced
- 2 tablespoons hot paprika, hungarian
- 1/2 teaspoon dried marjoram
- 2 lbs sauerkraut, rinsed,squeezed dry
- 1 cup sour cream
- 1 teaspoon caraway seed
- salt
- cooked hot buttered noodles

Direction

- In a Dutch oven heat oil and brown the meat on all sides, when browned set aside.
- Add onions to the skillet, sauté 5 minutes.
- Pour off excess fat and return meat to the pot.
- Sprinkle in the paprika and Marjoram.
- Top with sauerkraut.
- Bake covered for 1-hour 350F degrees oven.
- Add salt.
- When ready to serve stir in the sour cream and caraway seeds.
- Serve over hot buttered noodles.

Nutrition Information

- Calories: 806.9
- Total Fat: 71
- Saturated Fat: 29.5
- Fiber: 6
- Sugar: 5.8
- Cholesterol: 158.3
- Protein: 30
- Sodium: 1095.4
- Total Carbohydrate: 12.4

63. Hungarian Green Pepper Stew (Aka: Letcho)

Serving: 4-6 serving(s) | Prep: 30mins | Ready in:

Ingredients

- 3 lbs green peppers or 3 lbs yellow peppers, but not bells, quartered
- 1 large tomatoes, peeled and cut into 8 pieces
- 1 large onion, diced
- 3 -4 tablespoons oil
- 2 slices bacon (optional)
- 1 teaspoon salt
- 1 teaspoon paprika
- black pepper
- 1 garlic clove, minced (optional)
- 1/2 teaspoon caraway seed (optional)

Direction

- Cut bacon slices into smaller pieces and fry them in the same pot you're going to use for cooking the stew.
- Add and heat oil.
- Add diced onions. Cook onions on medium high heat until caramelized. Stir frequently, don't let them burn.
- As soon as the onions are done, add the peppers.
- Add salt, black pepper, garlic, caraway seeds and paprika.
- Stirring constantly, cook for a couple of minutes.
- Add tomatoes.
- Add a cup of water.
- Cover pot and simmer until peppers are done to your taste, 10-20 minutes.
- Add more salt and black pepper if needed.
- You might also have to add more water during the cooking process or evaporate extra liquid at the end. This depends on how juicy the tomato was and, on the way, you're going to serve the dish.

- If you like sausages, add about 1 lb. of sliced Polish Sausages or mini-smokes to the browned onions. Do not use uncooked sausages.
- Stir and fry sausages for 5 minutes before adding the peppers. Add less salt to the dish.
- You can thicken the stew with one or two eggs (scramble them first) at the end of the cooking process. Mix well.

Nutrition Information

- Calories: 183.8
- Protein: 3.8
- Fiber: 7.1
- Sugar: 11
- Sodium: 595.2
- Total Carbohydrate: 21.7
- Cholesterol: 0
- Total Fat: 11
- Saturated Fat: 1.6

64. Hungarian Grilled Cheese Sandwich

Serving: 4 serving(s) | Prep: 10mins | Ready in:

Ingredients

- 1 baguette
- 4 ounces swiss cheese, sliced
- 8 sour dill pickles, thinly sliced
- 8 slices Hungarian Salami, mild or spicy
- 1/2 teaspoon Hungarian paprika

Direction

- Cut baguette in half, lengthwise and partway through.
- Fill baguette with cheese, pickles and salami. Sprinkle with paprika and close.
- Cut baguette sandwich into 4.
- Heat skillet over medium-low heat and cook all 4 parts, approximately 8 minutes on each

side, while applying pressure on them, until cheese is melted and baguette is crispy and browned.

Nutrition Information

- Calories: 862.9
- Sugar: 8.3
- Total Carbohydrate: 149.1
- Cholesterol: 26.1
- Total Fat: 12.9
- Sodium: 2938.4
- Fiber: 7.8
- Protein: 38.2
- Saturated Fat: 6.4

65. Hungarian Halousky

Serving: 4-6 serving(s) | Prep: 20mins | Ready in:

Ingredients

- 1 large potato, boiled, peeled and grated
- 3 eggs, beaten
- 1 cup potato flour or 1 cup all-purpose flour
- salt and pepper, to taste
- dill weed, to taste
- water, to boil
- 16 ounces low fat cottage cheese or 16 ounces boiled cabbage, diced

Direction

- Fill a large pot with water and bring to a boil.
- In the meantime, in another pot, boil, peel and grate a large starchy potato.
- Combine potato with eggs, flour, salt, and pepper.
- Drop potato mixture by half teaspoons into the pot of boiling water.
- Dumplings are done when they float.
- When dumplings are done, remove them from the pot, drain the water, and return them to the pot.

- Sprinkle dumplings with dill then stir them with cottage cheese or cabbage.
- Re-warm to eating temperature and serve.

Nutrition Information

- Calories: 370.7
- Saturated Fat: 2.6
- Sodium: 538.8
- Fiber: 4.4
- Total Carbohydrate: 53.7
- Total Fat: 6.1
- Sugar: 2.8
- Cholesterol: 167.7
- Protein: 24.9

66. Hungarian Honey Cakes (Mézeskalács)

Serving: 24-48 cookies, 24-48 serving(s) | Prep: 24hours | Ready in:

Ingredients

- 4 cups flour
- 1 cup granulated sugar
- 2/3 cup honey
- 1/2 cup unsalted butter (4 TBSP or 2 ounces)
- 1 teaspoon ground cinnamon
- 1 teaspoon ground cloves
- 4 teaspoons baking soda
- 1 lemon, rind of, grated
- 1 egg
- BAKING AND PRE-BAKING DECORATION
- extra egg(s) for egg wash
- 3 drops red food coloring (optional)
- poppy seed (optional)
- COLORED SUGAR ICING
- 1 egg white
- powdered sugar, sifted (as much as needed to make fairly stiff paste)
- 3 drops food coloring, of choice

Direction

- DAY BEFORE BAKING:
- Sift together the flour, sugar, cinnamon, cloves and baking soda.
- Melt together the butter and the honey, pour over the flour combination and stir to mix.
- Add 1 egg and knead together. The dough should be soft (you can add a bit of lukewarm water if necessary), since it will harden a bit during its resting period.
- Cover the dough in a bowl and let it rest at least one day at room temperature.
- BAKING DAY:
- Rolling out the dough is easiest between two pieces of waxed paper.
- Cut desired shapes out of the dough (of about 3/8 inches thickness on average).
- Before baking, brush with the yolk of an egg to which a few drops of red food coloring have been added. If you are decorating with seeds, brush dough with egg white to "paste" seeds on top of dough before baking.
- (Alternately, let the honey cakes rest a few days and then decorate with colored sugar icings.).
- Place cut out pieces of dough on a cold, greased cookie sheet, bake at 350 degrees F. (or less) for about 6-8 minutes. Thicker pieces may need a longer time (ovens temperatures also vary).
- DECORATION:
- If icing cookies, let the honey cakes rest a few days and then decorate with colored sugar icings.
- MAKE VARIOUS COLORED SUGAR ICINGS:
- Colored sugar icing, one version: To one egg white, add as much sifted powdered sugar as needed to make fairly stiff paste. Add desired food colorings, separated by color. (Do not use a mixer!)
- Spoon this mixture into a small nylon baggie, cut a tiny hole in one corner, roll up and use like a pencil to draw and color.

Nutrition Information

- Calories: 175
- Fiber: 0.7
- Protein: 2.6
- Cholesterol: 19
- Total Fat: 4.3
- Saturated Fat: 2.5
- Sodium: 216.5
- Sugar: 16.1
- Total Carbohydrate: 32.1

67. Hungarian Hot Stew "hunky Stew"

Serving: 1 stew, 8 serving(s) | Prep: 20mins | Ready in:

Ingredients

- 3 lbs chuck roast
- 1/2 tablespoon hot pepper flakes
- 5 carrots, cut into large pieces (about 4 chunks per carrot depending on size)
- 3 celery, cut into large pieces
- 2 green bell peppers, cut into wedges
- 1 large onion, cut into wedges
- 1/2 tablespoon hot pepper flakes
- 5 russet potatoes, cut into large chunks (quartered or so depending on size)
- 2 (15 ounce) cans green beans, drained
- 2 teaspoons garlic salt
- 2 teaspoons salt
- 2 teaspoons pepper
- 1 (48 ounce) can tomato juice
- 2 (32 ounce) cans tomato sauce

Direction

- Cut meat into 2-3" chunks and put into a large pot or Dutch oven. Sprinkle with hot pepper seeds-to taste.
- Layer all of the ingredients in the order given, just make sure the tomato juice and sauce cover the veggies but not so much it becomes a soup. Wiggle the pan so the sauce distributes throughout.

- Cook on medium to medium-low heat for 1 hour, skimming when needed and stirring occasionally (at this point you want to stir carefully so as not to disrupt the layering too much).
- Cook an additional hour or so on medium-low or until the carrots are done.
- Serve with crusty bread (for sopping-very important!) and salad.

Nutrition Information

- Calories: 704.5
- Total Fat: 34.4
- Saturated Fat: 13.7
- Sodium: 2403.8
- Sugar: 22.1
- Total Carbohydrate: 62.7
- Fiber: 12.8
- Cholesterol: 117.4
- Protein: 41.2

68. Hungarian Lentil Stew

Serving: 8-10 serving(s) | Prep: 10mins | Ready in:

Ingredients

- 1 lb brown lentils
- 1 1/2 tablespoons vegetable oil
- 1 medium onion, finely chopped
- 6 garlic cloves, minced
- 2 tablespoons sweet Hungarian paprika
- 3 bay leaves
- 2 cups sour cream
- 3 1/2 tablespoons flour
- 2 tablespoons milk
- 1/2 teaspoon salt (to taste)
- 1 tablespoon light brown sugar
- 2 tablespoons brown mustard (to taste)
- 2 tablespoons lemon juice (to taste)

Direction

- If desired, soak lentils overnight. This step may be skipped but it makes the lentils more digestible.
- Place a large (5-6 quart) saucepan over medium-low heat, add oil and onions and sauté onions until tender, about 2 minutes.
- Add garlic and paprika, and sauté about another minute.
- Add lentils, 7 cups of water and bay leaves. Increase heat to a boil, then reduce heat to low. Cover and simmer, stirring occasionally, until lentils are tender, about 50 minutes. Add water as needed if mixture seems too thick.
- In a small bowl combine sour cream (not low fat), flour and milk. When lentils are tender add this mixture to the pot. Simmer 2-3 minutes. Add salt, brown sugar, mustard and lemon juice.

Nutrition Information

- Calories: 382.4
- Total Carbohydrate: 44.5
- Protein: 17.5
- Total Fat: 15.6
- Fiber: 18.3
- Sodium: 183.3
- Sugar: 3.8
- Cholesterol: 25.8
- Saturated Fat: 8.1

69. Hungarian Mushroom Stew

Serving: 4 serving(s) | Prep: 15mins | Ready in:

Ingredients

- 2 -4 tablespoons butter
- 2 medium onions, chopped
- 5 cups button mushrooms
- 1 green pepper, chopped and seeded
- 1 red pepper, chopped and seeded
- 3 garlic cloves, minced

- 2 1/2-3 1/2 teaspoons paprika, depending on how spicy you want it
- salt freshly ground black pepper, to taste
- optional cayenne pepper, to taste
- 1 teaspoon sugar
- 2 cups diced tomatoes, including their liquid
- 2 tablespoons red wine
- dumplings or noodles

Direction

- Melt butter in frying pan, add onions, and sauté until tender.
- Add mushrooms and sauté for a few more minutes, adding more butter if needed.
- Add peppers and sauté 5 minutes, until mushrooms are soft and brown.
- Add garlic and sauté another 2 minutes.
- Add spices, sugar, tomatoes and red wine and simmer for 30 minutes, stirring occasionally.
- Serve over dumplings or noodles.

Nutrition Information

- Calories: 141.1
- Protein: 5.1
- Total Fat: 6.6
- Total Carbohydrate: 17.4
- Cholesterol: 15.3
- Saturated Fat: 3.6
- Sodium: 65.5
- Fiber: 4.6
- Sugar: 9.7

70. Hungarian Nokedli (Dumplings)

Serving: 4 serving(s) | Prep: 10mins | Ready in:

Ingredients

- 2 eggs
- 1/2 teaspoon salt
- 3/4 cup water

- 2 cups all-purpose flour
- 1 large pot filled with salted boiling water

Direction

- Place large pot filled with salted water and bring to boil.
- Combine eggs, salt, and water, beating well with whisk.
- Add flour, a little at a time.
- Add only enough flour to make a soft, sticky dough.
- Let mixture rest for about 10 mins.
- Beat mixture again.
- Using the side of a teaspoon, spoon small amount of dough into boiling water.
- Dipping the spoon in the hot water will remove the dough from the spoon (if you have a spaetzle maker, that makes is easier as you want very small noodles).
- The noodles are done when they float to the top.
- Remove from water with large slotted spoon, and place in colander.
- Rinse with cold water.
- You may want to make the dumplings in 2 or 3 batches so they don't overcook.
- Serve with chicken paprikash.
- The dumplings are also nice added to a stew.
- You can heat the dumplings in a frying pan with melted butter.
- Do not let the dumplings get too brown or crisp.

Nutrition Information

- Calories: 263.2
- Fiber: 1.7
- Sugar: 0.3
- Cholesterol: 93
- Total Fat: 3
- Saturated Fat: 0.9
- Sodium: 328.8
- Total Carbohydrate: 47.9
- Protein: 9.6

71. Hungarian Noodles With Vegetarian Sausage

Serving: 4 serving(s) | Prep: 15mins | Ready in:

Ingredients

- 3 tablespoons olive oil
- 6 -8 vegetarian sausages (MorningStar or Boca are good)
- 1 large sweet onion, quartered and thinly sliced
- 1 (16 ounce) packageshredded mixed cabbage (or 1 lb. you shred yourself)
- 3⁄4 cup vegetable broth
- 8 ounces wide egg noodles, yolk-free if desired (6 1/2 cups)
- 2 tablespoons chopped fresh parsley
- 1 tablespoon poppy seed, as desired
- paprika

Direction

- Bring large pot of lightly salted water to a boil for noodles.
- Meanwhile, in large, wide skillet, heat 1 tablespoon oil over medium heat.
- Add veg.
- Sausage and cook, turning often, until browned on all sides, about 7 minutes.
- Transfer to plate.
- In same skillet, heat remaining 2 tablespoons oil over medium heat.
- Add onion, and cook, stirring often, until golden, about 8 minutes.
- Stir in cabbage and broth.
- Cover and cook, stirring occasionally, until cabbage is wilted and just beginning to brown lightly, about 10 to 12 minutes.
- While cabbage is cooking, add noodles to boiling water.
- Cook until just tender, about 10 minutes.
- Cut veg.
- Sausage into 1/2-inch-thick rounds.
- Drain noodles well.

- Transfer to large serving dish.
- Add cooked cabbage, veg.
- Sausage slices, parsley, poppy seeds, 1/2 teaspoon salt and 1/2 teaspoon freshly ground pepper.
- Toss gently but thoroughly to combine. Sprinkle with paprika to taste.
- Serve hot. Enjoy!
- Enjoy!

Nutrition Information

- Calories: 460.4
- Sugar: 6.4
- Cholesterol: 47.9
- Protein: 17.3
- Total Fat: 20.6
- Fiber: 6.9
- Saturated Fat: 3.3
- Sodium: 368.7
- Total Carbohydrate: 55.1

72. Hungarian Nut Crescents

Serving: 120 cresents | Prep: 24hours | Ready in:

Ingredients

- pastry dough
- 1 cup butter
- 1 cup shortening
- 6 1/4 cups flour
- 2 tablespoons yeast
- 1 pint sour cream
- 3 egg yolks
- 1 pinch salt
- FILLING
- 1/2 lb ground walnuts
- 1 1/4 cups sugar
- 1/4 teaspoon cinnamon
- 1 teaspoon vanilla
- 3 egg whites, stiffly beaten
- EGG WASH

- 1 egg yolk
- 3 -5 drops water
- extra sugar

Direction

- In a bowl, cut the butter and shortening into the flour until the mixture is crumbly.
- In a separate bowl, mix the yeast into sour cream, then add egg yolks and salt.
- Combine with the flour mixture.
- Mix until smooth and the sides of the bowl are clean.
- Form into a large ball and chill, covered, overnight.
- To make filling, mix walnuts, sugar, cinnamon, vanilla and stiffly beaten egg whites together in a bowl.
- To make egg wash mix egg yolk and few drops of water in a small bowl.
- Preheat oven to 350°.
- Sprinkle granulated sugar onto a pastry board.
- Divide the dough into six portions.
- Work with one portion at a time, refrigerating the dough you are not using.
- Roll out the dough to 1/8-inch thick and sprinkle with more sugar.
- Cut into 2 x 2-inch squares.
- Place a bit of the nut filling along one end of the square and roll up.
- Form into a crescent.
- Place seam side down on a greased cookie sheet.
- Paint with egg wash.
- Bake at 350° for 15-20 minutes.
- Remove from oven and cool on wire racks.

Nutrition Information

- Calories: 83.8
- Saturated Fat: 2.1
- Fiber: 0.3
- Total Carbohydrate: 7.6
- Protein: 1.4
- Sodium: 16.2
- Sugar: 2.2

- Cholesterol: 12.1
- Total Fat: 5.5

73. Hungarian Nut Nuggets (Cookies)

Serving: 60-70 cookies | Prep: 20mins | Ready in:

Ingredients

- 1 lb butter, room temperature
- 10 tablespoons powdered sugar
- 2 cups of medium-coarse chopped walnuts
- 2 teaspoons vanilla extract
- 4 cups flour

Direction

- In a large bowl blend the ingredients with a wire pastry blender until the ingredients form when squeezed together.
- Form into balls (or nuggets) by tablespoons; dough will be very crumbly; I press and form them in my palms instead of my fingers.
- Place on a cookie sheet and bake at 350 degrees for about 10 minutes until they start to brown around edges.
- Watch them so they do not burn.
- Cool and roll in powdered sugar.
- Store in cool place until serving.

Nutrition Information

- Calories: 115.7
- Cholesterol: 16.3
- Total Fat: 8.8
- Saturated Fat: 4.1
- Total Carbohydrate: 8.2
- Protein: 1.5
- Sodium: 43.9
- Fiber: 0.5
- Sugar: 1.4

74. Hungarian Paprika Potato Soup

Serving: 4 serving(s) | Prep: 15mins | Ready in:

Ingredients

- 2 lbs russet potatoes, peeled and cut into 3 inch cubes
- 4 cups low sodium chicken broth or 4 cups vegetable broth
- 1 tablespoon smoky paprika
- 1 teaspoon hot paprika
- 1 teaspoon celery seed
- 1/2 teaspoon salt
- 1 tablespoon olive oil
- 1 white onion, finely chopped
- 2 tablespoons finely chopped fresh dill
- 1/8 teaspoon ground nutmeg
- 1 cup nonfat milk

Direction

- Place potatoes, broth, paprika, celery seeds, and salt in 4-quart or larger slow cooker. Stir to combine.
- Heat oil in medium skillet over medium-high heat. Add onion and sauté until translucent, about 5 minutes. Transfer to cooker.
- Cover. Cook on low 4 to 6 hours, or until potatoes are tender. Stir to break up potatoes into broth for a slightly chunky consistency.
- Add dill, nutmeg, and freshly ground black pepper to taste. Stir in milk. Cover. Cook 20 to 30 more minutes, or until heated through.

Nutrition Information

- Calories: 285.1
- Sodium: 410.8
- Fiber: 6.3
- Total Carbohydrate: 49.8
- Cholesterol: 1.2
- Total Fat: 5.6
- Saturated Fat: 1.1
- Protein: 12.2

- Sugar: 6.6

75. Hungarian Pastry

Serving: 16 serving(s) | Prep: 20mins | Ready in:

Ingredients

- 1/4 lb butter (I use butter) or 1/4 lb margarine (I use butter)
- 1/2 cup sugar
- 1 teaspoon vanilla
- 2 eggs, separated
- 1 1/2 cups flour
- 1 pinch baking soda
- 1/2 teaspoon baking powder
- jam (I use raspberry)
- 1 cup ground nuts (I use walnuts)
- 2 tablespoons sugar

Direction

- Cream butter/margarine and sugar.
- Add vanilla and egg yolks.
- Cream together well.
- Add sifted flour with soda and baking powder.
- Mix well.
- Then pat dough out onto cookie sheet with sides or a large shallow pan.
- Spread with jam and 1/2 cup ground nuts.
- Then over that spread the well beaten egg whites.
- Then sprinkle the other half of ground nuts to which 2 tablespoons of sugar have been added.
- Bake 1/2 hour at 325 degrees Fahrenheit.
- Layers are:
- Dough.
- Jam.
- Nuts.
- Egg whites.
- Nuts with sugar.
- When cool, cut into 2-inch squares.

Nutrition Information

- Calories: 133.8
- Cholesterol: 41.7
- Fiber: 0.3
- Total Carbohydrate: 16.9
- Sugar: 7.9
- Protein: 2.1
- Total Fat: 6.5
- Saturated Fat: 3.9
- Sodium: 65.2

76. Hungarian Pigs In Blanket

Serving: 8 serving(s) | Prep: 0S | Ready in:

Ingredients

- 1 large head cabbage
- 2 lbs ground pork
- 1 cup uncooked rice
- 1 onion
- 3 tablespoons paprika
- salt
- 1 (16 ounce) can tomato juice
- 1 (16 ounce) can sauerkraut

Direction

- Steam cabbage until soft enough to fold.
- Mix onion rice pork paprika and salt. Place small amount of mixture on each cabbage leaf and roll tightly.
- In a large pan alternate layers of sauerkraut and cabbage rolls. Cover all with tomato juice.
- Cook @ 350 2-3 hours.

Nutrition Information

- Calories: 496.8
- Sodium: 663.4
- Sugar: 9.6
- Protein: 34.5
- Saturated Fat: 8.9

- Fiber: 6.8
- Total Carbohydrate: 35.9
- Cholesterol: 106.7
- Total Fat: 24.4

77. Hungarian Pork And Lentil Stew

Serving: 6 serving(s) | Prep: 20mins | Ready in:

Ingredients

- 1 tablespoon olive oil
- 2 onions, chopped
- 500 g lean pork, diced
- 2 teaspoons sweet Hungarian paprika
- 1 teaspoon hot paprika
- 60 g red lentils
- 1/2 teaspoon dried thyme
- 2 tablespoons tomato paste
- 2 teaspoons soft brown sugar
- 375 ml beef stock
- 1 tomatoes, to garnish
- 2 tablespoons low-fat yogurt
- salt and black pepper

Direction

- In a large, deep saucepan, heat the olive oil over the high heat. Add in the onion, pork, hot and Hungarian paprika. Stir until browned. It should take about 4 minutes.
- Add in the lentils, thyme, tomato paste, sugar, stock. Season to taste. Bring the mixture to a boil.
- Lower the heat to very minimal. Cover with lid and cook, for approximately 18 minutes, stirring occasionally.
- Uncover and cook for further 25 minutes. Make sure it becomes thick. Remove from the heat, then set aside for about 8 minutes.
- Meanwhile, prepare the tomato. By using a sharp knife, cut the tomato in half, then remove the seeds. Slice the flesh into thin strips.

- To serve, stir in the yoghurt to the stew. Scatter with tomato. To better fill your stomach, serve with some rice.

Nutrition Information

- Calories: 213
- Sugar: 4.7
- Total Carbohydrate: 13.7
- Cholesterol: 49.5
- Fiber: 2.6
- Sodium: 316.8
- Protein: 22.3
- Total Fat: 7.7
- Saturated Fat: 2.1

78. Hungarian Pot Roast

Serving: 8 serving(s) | Prep: 25mins | Ready in:

Ingredients

- 3 -4 lbs chuck roast
- 1/4 cup flour, and
- 2 tablespoons flour
- 1 tablespoon salt
- 1/4 teaspoon ground pepper
- 3 tablespoons bacon drippings or 3 tablespoons butter or 3 tablespoons vegetable oil
- 1 garlic clove, crushed
- 1 large onion, sliced
- celery
- 1/2 cup beef broth
- 1 (8 ounce) can tomato sauce
- 1/2 cup sour cream
- 3 tablespoons parsley, chopped
- 8 ounces wide egg noodles, cooked and drained

Direction

- Mix flour, salt and pepper.
- Dredge meat in flour mixture.

- Brown meat in bacon drippings on both sides.
- Pour off excess drippings.
- Add garlic, onion, celery, broth and tomato sauce.
- Cover tightly and simmer 3 to 3-1/2 hours or until tender.
- Remove roast to a heated platter.
- Mix in the sour cream and parsley, NEVER ALLOWING IT TO BOIL.
- Surround roast with noodles and pour sour cream gravy over all.

Nutrition Information

- Calories: 657.8
- Sodium: 1180.4
- Total Carbohydrate: 29.7
- Cholesterol: 152.3
- Protein: 37.1
- Saturated Fat: 17.6
- Fiber: 1.9
- Sugar: 2.6
- Total Fat: 42.6

79. Hungarian Potato And Egg Casserole

Serving: 8 serving(s) | Prep: 15mins | Ready in:

Ingredients

- 2 lbs potatoes
- 1 onion, chopped
- 2 tablespoons oil
- 1 cup sour cream
- 1 1/2 teaspoons salt
- 1/4 teaspoon pepper
- 2 eggs, boiled and sliced
- 2 tablespoons dry breadcrumbs (or matzah meal)
- Hungarian paprika

Direction

- Do not peel or slice the potatoes.
- You will be cooking them whole.
- Heat salted water (1/2 teaspoons salt to 1 cup water) to boiling.
- Add potatoes.
- Heat to boiling.
- Reduce heat.
- Cover and cook until tender.
- Test with a fork or a knife for tenderness.
- Drain and cool slightly.
- Cook onion in oil until tender.
- Mix onion, oil, sour cream, salt and pepper.
- Peel potatoes and cut into 1/4 inch slices.
- Gently mix potatoes and sour cream mixture.
- Arrange half the potatoes in greased 10 x 6 x 1 1/2 inch baking dish or 1 1/2 quart casserole.
- Arrange eggs on top and add remaining potatoes.
- Sprinkle with bread crumbs and paprika.
- Bake, uncovered, at 325 degrees until light brown, 30 to 40 minutes.
- Garnish with snipped parsley if desired.

Nutrition Information

- Calories: 209.8
- Saturated Fat: 4.6
- Sodium: 488.1
- Protein: 5.1
- Total Fat: 10.9
- Total Carbohydrate: 23.8
- Cholesterol: 65.5
- Fiber: 2.8
- Sugar: 1.7

80. Hungarian Sausage

Serving: 4 1/2 pounds, 1 serving(s) | Prep: 30mins | Ready in:

Ingredients

- 3 lbs boneless pork butt, cut into large pieces
- 1 lb beef chuck, cut into large pieces

- 1 lb fresh pork fat, cut into large pieces
- 10 garlic cloves, peeled and crushed (about 2 Tablespoons)
- 1 cup water
- 2 tablespoons salt
- 1/2 tablespoon fresh ground black pepper
- 3 tablespoons Hungarian paprika
- 1 teaspoon saltpeter
- 1/4 teaspoon ground cloves
- pork sausage casing, about 10 feet, 1 inch in diameter as for Polish sausage

Direction

- In a meat grinder, coarsely grind the pork, beef, and pork fat, in batches. Add all the remaining ingredients except the casings. Mix well and allow to sit while you clean the casings.
- Rinse the casings thoroughly in cold water and run fresh water through them. Drain. Using a sausage machine, a KitchenAid with a sausage attachment, or a sausage funnel, fill the casings and tie them off into about 16-inch lengths. Do not fill them too tightly as they must have room to expand when they cook.
- Hang the sausages in a home-style smoker and smoke them for about one hour. Do not allow the temperature of the smoker to go above 150.
- Remove the sausages and hang over a stick or dowel. Put the stick in a cool place and position an electric fan so that it will blow directly on the sausages. Allow them to dry for two days. They are ready for use. Place them in the refrigerator, where they will keep well for about a week.

Nutrition Information

- Calories: 8396.4
- Sodium: 15070.2
- Sugar: 2.5
- Cholesterol: 1707.1
- Protein: 343.8
- Total Fat: 760.4
- Saturated Fat: 337.1

- Fiber: 9.4
- Total Carbohydrate: 23.8

81. Hungarian Sirloin With Mushroom Crepes

Serving: 6 serving(s) | Prep: 15mins | Ready in:

Ingredients

- 12 cooked, warm crepes (see recipe19104)
- 2 teaspoons lite olive oil
- 1 medium onion, chopped
- 1 tablespoon parsley, chopped
- 1/2 teaspoon salt
- 1 teaspoon paprika
- 1/4 teaspoon pepper
- 1 lb top sirloin steak, cut into thin strips (like stir fry cut)
- 1/2 lb mushroom, sliced
- 1 cup sour cream

Direction

- Have your sirloin half frozen to slice easily.
- Heat oil in the skillet, add onion and cook until the onion is translucent.
- Stir in the parsley, salt paprika, pepper steak.
- Cover and cook until the meat is tender.
- Add mushrooms, cook for 3 minutes.
- Stir in the sour cream.
- Divide between the 12 warm crepes, fold the crepes over serve immediately.

Nutrition Information

- Calories: 359.1
- Sodium: 270
- Fiber: 0.8
- Sugar: 1.5
- Total Carbohydrate: 5
- Cholesterol: 90.9
- Protein: 23.9
- Total Fat: 27

- Saturated Fat: 12

- Sodium: 147.5

82. Hungarian Spatzle

Serving: 8 serving(s) | Prep: 15mins | Ready in:

Ingredients

- 2 cups whole wheat flour
- 1 cup milk
- 2 eggs
- 1/4 cup butter, melted
- 1/4 teaspoon salt
- 1 pinch nutmeg (optional)
- salt pepper

Direction

- Whisk together the flour, milk, eggs, 1tbsp butter, salt nutmeg if using, Blend until the batter is smooth (use your blender).
- Let the batter rest for 30 minutes.
- Set a colander over a pot of boiling water.
- Put half the batter into the colander and with a wooden spoon push the batter through the colander and into the boiling water.
- The size of the spätzle depends on how fast you push it through the colander.
- Reduce heat, cover and simmer for 8 minutes.
- Transfer the spätzle to a heated bowl, cook remaining half.
- Toss with remaining butter.
- Season, Serve.

Nutrition Information

- Calories: 190.5
- Protein: 6.7
- Total Fat: 8.7
- Sugar: 0.2
- Total Carbohydrate: 23.3
- Fiber: 3.7
- Cholesterol: 72.4
- Saturated Fat: 4.8

83. Hungarian Split Pea Soup

Serving: 6 serving(s) | Prep: 30mins | Ready in:

Ingredients

- 1 lb yellow split peas
- 1 small ham shank or 1 small a 1 lb smoked pork butt
- 1 large onion, chopped
- 4 medium carrots, sliced
- 3 celery ribs, diced
- 1 parsley root, diced
- 1/4 cup chopped flat leaf parsley
- 1 parsnip, root diced
- 1 bay leaf
- 2 whole cloves
- 6 peppercorns
- 3 quarts water
- 1/4 cup pearl barley, -optional-

Direction

- Wash and drain yellow peas and place in soup pot with 3 quarts of cold water.
- Add ham or pork butt, along with vegetables and spices and optional barley.
- Bring water to a boil, turn down heat and slowly cook until all veggies and peas are soft.
- Taste for seasoning, and now add required salt. (Ham and pork butt are salty, do not add salt at the beginning of cooking).
- Cooking will take about an hour and a half.
- If the soup is not as thick as you like it, cook it a little longer. The soup should be quite thick.
- Serve in a large bowl with a slice of ham or pork butt in each serving.
- Add some crusty bread and a brisk light salad for a satisfying meal.

Nutrition Information

- Calories: 332.9
- Sodium: 76.2
- Sugar: 10.3
- Total Carbohydrate: 62.6
- Total Fat: 1.3
- Fiber: 23.6
- Cholesterol: 0
- Protein: 20.5
- Saturated Fat: 0.2

84. Hungarian Sponge Cake (Piskota Torta)

Serving: 8 serving(s) | Prep: 15mins | Ready in:

Ingredients

- 8 eggs, at room temperature separated
- 1/2 cup sugar
- 1/2 cup sifted cake flour
- 1 tablespoon lemon juice (I like the vanilla) or 1 tablespoon good vanilla extract (I like the vanilla)
- 1 teaspoon baking powder
- 1/4 teaspoon salt

Direction

- Preheat oven to 325F.
- Beat egg yolks until light yellow medium mixing bowl.
- Add sugar, lemon juice (or vanilla), and mix until thick.
- Add baking powder and flour gradually and mix well.
- In a clean bowl beat egg whites and salt until very stiff.
- Carefully fold egg whites into the yolk mixture.
- Grease and flour two 9" cake pans and pour batter evenly into them.
- Bake for one hour, remove from pans, and cool on cooling racks.

Nutrition Information

- Calories: 153.6
- Total Fat: 5
- Sugar: 12.9
- Cholesterol: 211.5
- Protein: 7
- Saturated Fat: 1.6
- Sodium: 188.2
- Fiber: 0.1
- Total Carbohydrate: 19.9

85. Hungarian Steak Soup

Serving: 6 serving(s) | Prep: 45mins | Ready in:

Ingredients

- 1 1/2 lbs boneless round steak, cut 3/4 inch thick
- 1 medium onion, preferably sweet such as vidalia
- 1 medium green pepper
- 1 medium red pepper
- 2 tablespoons vegetable oil
- 1 teaspoon Hungarian paprika
- 1/2 teaspoon Hungarian paprika
- 1/4 teaspoon fresh ground black pepper
- 1/2 teaspoon caraway seed, briefly toasted (see Note)
- 6 cups beef broth
- 2 bay leaves
- 1 tablespoon chopped garlic
- 2 teaspoons tomato paste
- 1 tablespoon salt
- 6 ounces wide egg noodles
- sour cream

Direction

- Pat the meat dry.
- Trim away any excess fat and cut the meat into 3/4-inch cubes.
- Cut the onion in half and coarsely chop one half.

- Thinly slice the other half and set aside.
- Core, seed, and cut the bell peppers in half.
- Cut one half of each pepper into chunks and the other half into 1/4-inch strips.
- Set aside.
- Heat oil in a pressure cooker or large heavy saucepan over medium-high heat until it shimmers, about 3 minutes.
- Ad half the meat and brown on all sides, about 4 minutes.
- Transfer to a bowl with a slotted spoon.
- Add the remaining meat and repeat.
- Add the chopped onion and bell pepper chunks to the pot.
- Stir frequently until the vegetables soften, 4 to 5 minutes.
- Add the sweet and hot paprika, black pepper and caraway seeds and stir for 1 minute.
- Pour in the beef broth.
- Add the bay leaves garlic, and tomato paste.
- Return the meat and accumulated juices to the pot.
- Cover and seal the pressure cooker, if using, and bring to full pressure over high heat.
- Regulate the heat and cook for 20 minutes.
- If using a saucepan, simmer partially covered for 1 to 1 1/2 hours.
- Release pressure and uncover the cooker.
- The meat should be cooked through and tender.
- If not, re-cover the pan, bring back to full pressure and cook for 5 minutes more.
- Pour the soup through a colander into a bowl, leaving as much of the meat as possible in the pot.
- Pick out the meat cubes in the colander and return to the pot.
- Discard the bay leaves and vegetables in the colander as well as any remaining in the pot.
- Add the onion slices and bell pepper strips to the pot and pour the broth back in over the vegetables and meat.
- Bring to a boil over high heat, reduce heat to low, and simmer, uncovered until the vegetables are just tender, 7 to 8 minutes.
- Meanwhile, bring water to a boil in a large saucepan.
- Add the salt and noodles and cook until the noodles are just tender.
- Drain the noodles.
- Spoon 1/2 cup of noodles into each of 6 soup bowls.
- Ladle the hot soup over the noodles and serve at once.
- Pass the sour cream at the table.
- Note: Toast the caraway seeds in a small skillet over medium-low heat, tossing often, until aromatic, about 5 minutes.

Nutrition Information

- Calories: 390.9
- Sodium: 1814.5
- Sugar: 2.9
- Protein: 31.2
- Total Fat: 18
- Saturated Fat: 5.4
- Total Carbohydrate: 25.5
- Cholesterol: 93.9
- Fiber: 2.3

86. Hungarian Style Spinach (Magyaros Spenotfozelek)

Serving: 4 serving(s) | Prep: 5mins | Ready in:

Ingredients

- 1 lb fresh spinach or 1 lb swiss chard, cooked, well drained and chopped
- 2 tablespoons butter
- 1 fresh garlic clove, finely chopped
- 2 tablespoons flour
- 1/4 teaspoon salt
- 1/8 teaspoon ground pepper
- 3/4 cup cream or 3/4 cup milk

Direction

- Melt butter in a small saucepan over low heat.
- Add garlic clove.
- Sauté garlic in butter a minute or so.
- Do not let garlic burn or it will be bitter.
- Blend in flour to make a roux.
- Add salt and pepper and heat until mixture bubbles, stirring constantly.
- Remove from heat.
- Gradually add cream or milk.
- Return to heat and stir until mixture is smooth and thickened.
- Blend well drained spinach into sauce and serve.

Nutrition Information

- Calories: 223.4
- Total Fat: 20.1
- Sodium: 291.4
- Fiber: 2.6
- Sugar: 0.6
- Total Carbohydrate: 8.7
- Saturated Fat: 12.4
- Cholesterol: 65
- Protein: 4.7

87. Hungarian Sweet And Sour Butter Beans

Serving: 12 serving(s) | Prep: 25mins | Ready in:

Ingredients

- 1 lb butter beans, soaked overnight
- salt
- 2 tablespoons oil or 2 tablespoons butter
- 3 tablespoons all-purpose flour
- 6 tablespoons vinegar
- 3 tablespoons sugar

Direction

- Cook the butter beans in boiling water (enough lightly salted water to cover) until done.
- In a saucepan, gently heat the 3 tablespoons oil or butter, once it is bubbling, add the flour and stir to make a paste or roux.
- Stir over the heat until the roux changes color to beige.
- Add the beans together with their cooking water, stirring constantly, to make a thickish sauce (add more water if necessary).
- Add the vinegar and sugar and stir until the sugar is dissolved.
- Taste and adjust flavor, if necessary, by adding more vinegar or sugar.
- Continue cooking, stirring, for a few more minutes.

Nutrition Information

- Calories: 67.3
- Sugar: 3.2
- Total Fat: 2.4
- Saturated Fat: 0.4
- Cholesterol: 0
- Protein: 1.7
- Sodium: 95.5
- Fiber: 1.4
- Total Carbohydrate: 9.6

88. Hungarian Tofu With Noodles

Serving: 2-3 , 2-3 serving(s) | Prep: 20mins | Ready in:

Ingredients

- 2 cups egg noodles, dry
- 1 (16 ounce) package tofu, drained
- 1 large Spanish onion, chopped (the yellow kind)
- 1 cup green cabbage (approx)
- 2 tablespoons olive oil
- 1 (8 ounce) can tomato sauce
- water (see directions)

- 1 teaspoon paprika (smoked for extra zing!)

Direction

- Boil a quart of salted water and cook the noodles for 8 minutes, you don't want them too soft. Drain and set aside.
- Cut the tofu into cubes or chunks of your liking, and drain well. Make sure all the excess water is out.
- Heat the oil in a heavy-bottomed pot and add the onion. Sauté until it starts to brown, about 10-15 minutes depending on how big you cut the pieces.
- Add the paprika and tomato sauce, mixing well. Add the tofu and cabbage.
- Fill the can from the sauce with water, and pour into the pot, mixing well.
- Bring the mixture to a boil, then let simmer on low heat for about 30-45 minutes, an hour if you really want the tofu and onions completely browned. Mix with the noodles for a complete meal!

Nutrition Information

- Calories: 473
- Sugar: 11.6
- Protein: 23.2
- Sodium: 635.3
- Fiber: 6
- Total Carbohydrate: 47
- Cholesterol: 31.9
- Total Fat: 24
- Saturated Fat: 3.6

89. Hungarian Vegetarian Cabbage Soup

Serving: 8 serving(s) | Prep: 5mins | Ready in:

Ingredients

- 1 (46 ounce) can tomato juice

- 4 cups shredded green cabbage (, 1 1/4 pounds - or more)
- 2 large carrots, shredded
- 1 cup thinly sliced celery
- 1 large onion, finely chopped
- salt and pepper
- caraway seed (optional)
- yogurt (optional)

Direction

- Combine everything except the caraway seeds and yogurt in a large pot.
- Bring to a boil, reduce heat, and simmer uncovered for an hour.
- When serving, garnish with yogurt and caraway seeds, if desired.

Nutrition Information

- Calories: 54.1
- Total Fat: 0.2
- Cholesterol: 0
- Protein: 2.2
- Saturated Fat: 0.1
- Sodium: 480
- Fiber: 2.6
- Sugar: 9
- Total Carbohydrate: 13

90. Incredible Seasoning Salt Recipe.

Serving: 3 1/2 cups, about | Prep: 10mins | Ready in:

Ingredients

- 26 ounces sea salt (one container)
- 1 -2 tablespoon ground dill seed (or 1 tbls. dill weed)
- 1 -2 tablespoon onion powder
- 2 -4 tablespoons ground celery seed
- 1 -2 tablespoon garlic powder
- 2 -4 tablespoons sweet Hungarian paprika

- 4 -6 tablespoons fresh ground black pepper
- 4 -6 tablespoons fresh ground white pepper
- 4 -8 tablespoons sugar
- 1 -2 tablespoon ground mace
- 1 -2 tablespoon curry powder (Maharajah style preferred)
- 1 -2 tablespoon mustard powder

Direction

- Mix half of the plain sea salt with the rest of the spices, and then add the remaining sea salt.
- Place in tight lidded container and shake it really well. Shake it once a day for the next week. It gets better with age and holds well for six months or more.
- This salt blend is excellent on meat, poultry, seafood, vegetables, and most anything.

Nutrition Information

- Calories: 378.6
- Total Fat: 17.1
- Saturated Fat: 1.7
- Sugar: 15.6
- Total Carbohydrate: 57.7
- Sodium: 82363.9
- Fiber: 14.3
- Cholesterol: 0
- Protein: 14.3

91. Italian Pizzelle Cookies

Serving: 48 serving(s) | Prep: 15mins | Ready in:

Ingredients

- 1 cup oleo or 1 cup butter
- 1 1/3 cups sugar
- 6 eggs
- 1 1/2 cups flour
- 1 1/2 teaspoons baking powder
- 1 ounce anise flavoring

Direction

- Melt oleo or butter and mix in sugar.
- Let mixture cool.
- Add eggs and flour.
- Add baking powder and anise flavoring.
- Add additional flour as needed to make soft dough.
- Refrigerate dough to make it easier to work with.
- Drop by spoonfuls onto your pizzelle iron.
- Cook 1 minute or until lightly golden brown.
- Let them cool before stacking, this will help make your cookies crisp.

Nutrition Information

- Calories: 78.8
- Total Fat: 4.4
- Saturated Fat: 0.9
- Fiber: 0.1
- Protein: 1.2
- Sodium: 64.5
- Sugar: 5.6
- Total Carbohydrate: 8.7
- Cholesterol: 26.4

92. Kiflie, Hungarian Cookies

Serving: 12 cookies per sheet. | Prep: 5mins | Ready in:

Ingredients

- 1 (17 ounce) package puff pastry sheets
- 1 cup grated walnuts
- 1/2 cup brown sugar
- 1/2 cup granulated sugar
- 1/2 cup heavy cream

Direction

- Lay out puff pastry on floured board.
- Combine grated walnuts and the sugars, mix thoroughly.

- Add cream until mixture is a thin paste, spreadable but not runny.
- Form cookies.
- Method 1. Spread filling on top of pastry, edge to edge in one direction but leave 1 inch uncovered on both edges in the other direction.
- Starting with an uncovered edge roll the pastry into a cylinder. Wet the uncovered edge when you reach it and seal it to the side.
- Place rolled dough in freezer for no more than 20 minutes to firm it for cutting.
- Cut dough cylinder into 1/2-inch circles and place on greased cookie sheet.
- Method 2. Cut pastry sheets into squares 2 inches by 2 inches.
- Place a 12 teaspoon of the filling into the center of the square and bring two opposite points of the square together over the top of the filling.
- Either method, bake cookies at 425 degrees Fahrenheit for 12 minutes.
- Allow to cool and enjoy.

Nutrition Information

- Calories: 386.1
- Total Fat: 25.3
- Sugar: 17.7
- Cholesterol: 13.6
- Saturated Fat: 6.8
- Sodium: 107.5
- Fiber: 1.3
- Total Carbohydrate: 37
- Protein: 4.6

93. Kiflies

Serving: 85 | Prep: 0S | Ready in:

Ingredients

- 3 cups unsifted flour
- 1/2 cup sour cream (plus 2 tablespoons)
- 8 medium egg yolks
- small lemon, rind of, grated (yellow part only)
- 1/2 tablespoon sugar
- 1/2 lb butter (or 1/4 lb butter + 1/4 lb margarine where you don't use all the margarine)
- Filling
- 1 lb walnuts, shelled, and ground fine
- 8 egg whites
- 1 lb confectioners' sugar
- 1 small lemon, juice of (about 2 tbsp)

Direction

- Mix flour and butter until mixture is like cornmeal.
- Beat together sour cream, egg yolks, lemon rind and sugar, add to flour mixture.
- Knead the dough until smooth and elastic. Dough will have a satiny appearance and all the dough will come off your hands. Knead at least 20 minutes. The longer you work the dough the flakier the finished product will be. Do not cheat on kneading time.
- Pinch off pieces of dough no larger than a walnut and form into balls. Place balls side by side in a cake pan. Separate layers with wax paper. This should make about 85 balls.
- Cover tightly with aluminum foil and refrigerate overnight. (Dough balls may be frozen for up to 6 months. Freezing seems to make the dough even more tender when baked. Thaw in refrigerator overnight, not at room temperature.)
- Remove 1 dozen balls from the refrigerator at a time. If dough is too warm or too cold it is difficult to roll out. Roll each ball into a 4" circle. Circles will be tissue paper thin. Use as little flour as possible to keep dough from sticking to pastry board. It is best to make a mixture of 6 tablespoons flour and 2 tablespoons confectioners' sugar for sprinkling the board.
- Lay rolled out circles of pastry on a large tray just barely overlapping so they will not stick together. Use waxed paper between layers. When a dozen balls have been rolled,

refrigerate the tray so dough does not become too soft. If this happens kieflies will not be attractive.

- It is easier to assemble if you roll out about 36 balls, fill and bake. All the balls may be rolled at one time, but keep pastry circles refrigerated until ready to fill. Work with only as many circles as will it a one cookie sheet at a time.
- To assemble kieflies, place a semi-heaping tablespoon of filling across the middle of each circle, but not quite to the edge. Fold 1/3 of the dough over filling, overlapping about half way; fold the remaining 1/3 of the dough so it overlaps the first 1/3. Use a gentle hand when overlapping the filling so that when it bakes the filling will have room to expand. Shape the rolls into crescents, using thumbs and fingers. When forming the crescents, the edges might curl up slightly. Do not try to smooth out the dough. To do so would not allow the dough to expand and become flaky.
- Always place filled kieflies on a cool, ungreased cookie sheet. Bake no more than 1 sheet at a time. Preheat oven to 400 degrees, reduce heat to 375 degrees and bake 10 to 12 minutes or only until lightly browned.
- While kieflies are still warm generously coat with confectioners' sugar by sprinkling it through a small sieve or shaker.
- Filling; beat egg whites until stiff peaks form. Gradually beat in confectioners' sugar and lemon juice. Use a spatula to fold in ground nuts until thoroughly blended. If filling seems a bit "weepy" add about 3 crushed graham crackers.
- NOTE Kieflies will keep up to a week if kept in a cool spot. DO NOT cover tightly.
- These kieflies freeze beautifully. They will thaw at room temperature (uncovered) in about 3 hours. Freshen with confectioners' sugar when ready to serve.

Nutrition Information

- Calories: 100.5
- Cholesterol: 24.1
- Total Fat: 6.4
- Saturated Fat: 2
- Fiber: 0.5
- Sugar: 5.5
- Total Carbohydrate: 9.8
- Sodium: 22.2
- Protein: 1.9

94. Krautfleckerl Hungarian Cabbage And Noodles

Serving: 6 serving(s) | Prep: 25mins | Ready in:

Ingredients

- 1 tablespoon salt
- 4 cups finely shredded cabbage (or grated)
- 1 cup finely sliced onion
- 4 tablespoons butter (vegetable oil or other fat)
- 2 teaspoons sugar
- 1/4 teaspoon pepper
- 3 cups cooked broad egg noodles, drained
- sour cream, to serve (optional)

Direction

- Mix the salt and cabbage together and let stand 30 minutes.
- Squeeze out as much liquid as possible. Heat the butter in a deep skillet, add the onions, cabbage, sugar and pepper.
- Cook over low heat, stirring frequently, until cabbage is browned, about 25/30 minutes.
- Add the noodles and toss to blend thoroughly.
- Note: To reduce fat, you can use just 1 tablespoon butter and sauté the cabbage for a few minutes, then finish with a little chicken stock, stirring frequently.

Nutrition Information

- Calories: 206.3
- Total Fat: 9.4

- Total Carbohydrate: 26.8
- Cholesterol: 43.5
- Protein: 4.6
- Saturated Fat: 5.2
- Sodium: 1243.8
- Fiber: 2.6
- Sugar: 4.3

---

95. Langos

Serving: 6-8 serving(s) | Prep: 35mins | Ready in:

Ingredients

- 3 -4 medium potatoes
- Yeast
- 1/2 cup warm milk, for yeast
- 1/2 teaspoon sugar
- 1 2/3 cups flour
- 1/2 teaspoon salt
- lard (for frying)

Direction

- Cook the potatoes in boiling salted water.
- Peel them and immediately mash them. You should have about 1 1/2 cups. Cool.
- Mix the warm milk with the yeast and sugar. Let the starter sit for 5 or 10 minutes.
- Mix mashed potatoes with flour and the salt. Start with 1 1/2 cups and add more flour to make a knead-able dough. Knead dough well.
- Put dough in a bowl and cover.
- Let dough rise in a warm place until double in bulk. About 1 hour.
- Roll out the dough with a floured rolling pin on a floured board to 1/2 inch thick.
- Cut into rectangles, squares or circles. Triangles were my favorite. Prick the center of the dough with two slits with a knife to keep big bubbles from forming.
- Melt Lard in a frying pan so it is at least 1/2 deep.
- Fry Langos over medium heat. If the lard is too hot, they will burn, if the lard is to cool the

Langos will absorb too much lard. You will have to watch them. Let them get a nice tannish/brown color.

- When they are done, rub each Langos with a cut clove of garlic and sprinkle with salt both sides.
- Serve warm. (Good to accompany with a cold beer).

Nutrition Information

- Calories: 222.8
- Protein: 6.4
- Sodium: 210.8
- Saturated Fat: 0.5
- Fiber: 3.3
- Sugar: 1.3
- Total Carbohydrate: 46.4
- Cholesterol: 2.9
- Total Fat: 1.2

---

96. Latvian Borscht(AKA Ukrainian Borshch)

Serving: 6-8 serving(s) | Prep: 24hours | Ready in:

Ingredients

- 8 cups beef stock
- 1/2 head cabbage, finely shredded (or equivalent amount of spinach)
- 3 medium potatoes, cut into 1 inch cubes
- 1 large red beet, shredded
- 1 tablespoon red wine vinegar
- 1 teaspoon bacon fat
- 2 teaspoons sugar
- 2 tablespoons butter
- 2 medium onions, finely chopped
- 2 peeled tomatoes, chopped (4 canned tomatoes are fine)
- 1 carrot, sliced
- 1 parsley roots or 1/2 parsnip
- 6 peppercorns

- 3 allspice berries
- 3 bay leaves
- 1 head garlic, peeled and chopped
- 2 tablespoons bacon fat
- fresh parsley, chopped
- Garnish
- sour cream

Direction

- Heat the stock in a large soup pot, add cabbage and potatoes and simmer for 15 minutes.
- In the meantime, mix the beets, vinegar, bacon fat, sugar, and tomatoes in a saucepan and cook gently, covered, for about 5 minutes.
- Set aside.
- Then, in another small pan, heat the butter, mix in the onion, carrot, and parsley root (or parsnip), and braise.
- When the cabbage and potatoes are finished simmering, add the beet mixture, the onion mixture, the peppercorns, allspice berries, and bay leaves--and cook another 10 minutes.
- Stir in the chopped garlic, the remaining bacon fat, and the chopped parsley.
- Then turn the heat down to a very low simmer, lightly cover the pot, and simmer very slowly for about 4½ hours.
- Turn off the heat, let cool, and allow to ripen for about 12-18 hours.
- When ready to serve, reheat gently then ladle into bowls.
- Top each with a teaspoonful of sour cream and serve with a slice of dark rye bread.

Nutrition Information

- Calories: 210.5
- Sodium: 1267.3
- Sugar: 8.8
- Total Fat: 4.9
- Saturated Fat: 2.9
- Protein: 8.5
- Fiber: 6.3
- Total Carbohydrate: 35.2

- Cholesterol: 10.2

97. Lazy Pierogie Casserole

Serving: 4-6 serving(s) | Prep: 15mins | Ready in:

Ingredients

- 15 lasagna noodles
- 2 eggs
- 2 cups cheddar cheese (shredded)
- 2 cups mashed potatoes
- pepper, to taste
- garlic salt, to taste
- onion powder, to taste
- 1 cup butter
- 1 onion, chopped
- sour cream

Direction

- Cook lasagna noodles and drain.
- Line bottom of 9x13 pan with a single layer of noodles.
- In bowl mix mashed potatoes, cheese, egg, and spices.
- Spread half over noodles.
- Cover with another layer of noodles, then potato mixture.
- Melt butter or margarine in fry pan, sauté onion until clear and soft.
- Pour over noodles.
- Cover with foil.
- Bake 30 minutes in 350F oven.
- Let stand 10 minutes before cutting.
- Serve with sour cream.

Nutrition Information

- Calories: 1087.2
- Sugar: 4.8
- Total Carbohydrate: 86
- Total Fat: 69.2
- Saturated Fat: 42.4

- Fiber: 4.7
- Protein: 31.1
- Sodium: 1035
- Cholesterol: 289.2

98. Lecso

Serving: 6-8 serving(s) | Prep: 45mins | Ready in:

Ingredients

- 2 tablespoons olive oil
- 2 tablespoons paprika
- 1 kg tomatoes
- 2 bell peppers
- 3 -4 banana peppers
- 3 large onions, sliced in 1/4-inch rounds
- 3⁄4 kg sausage (any kind will work)
- 200 g thick slab bacon
- 1 teaspoon salt
- 1⁄2 teaspoon pepper, to taste

Direction

- Sauté onions in olive oil. Add paprika and then add the rest of the ingredients.
- Slice tomatoes and peppers into cubes and when onions are translucent add them to the pan. Let cook on low heat for about 1/2 hour; add salt and pepper to taste.
- That is the basic recipe -- my mother always canned several jars and then used it with eggs scrambled in the sauce, or added potatoes or Nokedli Hungarian homemade noodles). You can also add Kolbaz or any kind of sausage or bacon you like.

Nutrition Information

- Calories: 675.2
- Saturated Fat: 18
- Fiber: 5.4
- Protein: 22.1
- Total Fat: 56.3

- Sodium: 1819.7
- Sugar: 9.2
- Total Carbohydrate: 21.8
- Cholesterol: 95.2

99. Lekvar Prune Plum Filling Or (Apricot)

Serving: 2 1/2 cups | Prep: 10mins | Ready in:

Ingredients

- 1 1/2 cups pitted prunes, lightly packed
- 2⁄3 cup water
- 1 teaspoon grated lemon rind
- 3 tablespoons lemon juice
- 1⁄3 cup brown sugar

Direction

- Simmer all ingredients, except brown sugar, covered 25- 30 minutes until very soft and most of water is evaporated.
- Uncover last few minutes if necessary.
- Remove from heat and mash.
- Stir in brown sugar.
- You can keep Lekvar in the refrigerator for a long time.
- Put it in a canning jar.

Nutrition Information

- Calories: 360.2
- Total Carbohydrate: 95.4
- Protein: 2.3
- Saturated Fat: 0.1
- Sugar: 67.6
- Sodium: 15
- Fiber: 7.4
- Cholesterol: 0
- Total Fat: 0.4

100. Linzer Meringue Cake (Linzer Teszta)

Serving: 16-20 serving(s) | Prep: 1hours | Ready in:

Ingredients

- 3 cups flour
- 1 teaspoon baking powder
- 2 tablespoons sugar
- 1/4 lb butter, chilled
- 1/4 lb shortening, chilled
- 1 1/3 cups you favorite jam, I like apricot, raspberry (or lekvar*) or 1 1/3 cups plums
- 5 eggs, separated
- 1 teaspoon vanilla extract
- 6 tablespoons sour cream
- 1 cup sugar
- 1/2 cup ground walnuts

Direction

- Sift first three ingredients together.
- Cut in the butter and shortening to the flour mixture.
- In a separate bowl, mix together the egg yolks, vanilla, and sour cream
- Add this mixture to the flour and butter mixture.
- Cover and refrigerate for 1 hour.
- Preheat oven to 350°F.
- On a floured surface, roll the chilled dough out to fit the bottom of an 11" x 15" x 1" baking pan (you may need to trim the edges but try not to make the dough too thin).
- Bake for 30 minutes.
- White cake is baking, beat, in a very clean bowl, the egg whites until stiff peaks form on the tips of the beaters, gradually adding the sugar while beating.
- Remove cake from oven and immediately spread with meringue.
- Sprinkle with walnuts and return to oven for about 15 minutes or until meringue is lightly browned (watch this very closely so it won't burn).

- Serve warm, room temp, or, my favorite, chilled.
- *lekvar is a European fruit jam that is thicker than American jams and has more of a texture like fruit butter.

Nutrition Information

- Calories: 377.3
- Saturated Fat: 6.7
- Sodium: 96.9
- Fiber: 1.1
- Sugar: 27.3
- Total Carbohydrate: 51.1
- Total Fat: 17.2
- Cholesterol: 83.3
- Protein: 5.1

101. Liptauer Cheese A La Nigella Lawson

Serving: 4 Cups | Prep: 20mins | Ready in:

Ingredients

- 18 ounces cream cheese
- 2 1/4 cups cottage cheese
- 4 -5 tablespoons capers
- 8 cornichons, chopped
- 3 teaspoons paprika
- 1 pinch salt
- 1 pinch black pepper
- 2 teaspoons caraway seeds
- 2 teaspoons French mustard
- 1 -2 tablespoon vegetable oil
- 1 pinch paprika

Direction

- Beat the cream cheese and cottage cheese together until they are very smooth. Add the capers, cornichons, paprika, salt, pepper, caraway seeds, and mustard. Mix together well and turn into a 1-quart bowl lined with plastic wrap for easier unmolding later. Smooth the top with a spatula and cover with the overhanging plastic wrap. Place it in the refrigerator to set.

- When it has become cold enough to turn out — a few hours should do it — unwrap the folded-over plastic wrap on top, place a plate over the now uncovered bowl, turn it over, and unmold. Pull the plastic wrap off and drizzle over a rust-red ooze made by mixing the oil with the paprika.
- Serve this with bread or poppy-seed bagels, gherkins, and, if you like, some chopped red onions.

Nutrition Information

- Calories: 609.5
- Total Fat: 53
- Sodium: 2705.8
- Sugar: 8.9
- Total Carbohydrate: 14.5
- Cholesterol: 160.7
- Saturated Fat: 27.3
- Fiber: 3
- Protein: 21.9

102. Liptoi Cheese Spread

Serving: 2 cups | Prep: 5mins | Ready in:

Ingredients

- 1/2 lb cottage cheese
- 1/4 lb butter, softened
- 1 tablespoon Hungarian paprika or 1 tablespoon regular paprika
- 1 teaspoon prepared mustard
- 1 teaspoon caraway seed
- 1 teaspoon minced capers
- 1 tablespoon grated onion
- 1/4 cup sour cream

Direction

- Mix butter with cottage cheese to blend well.
- Add remaining ingredients.
- Mix well again.
- Refrigerate for a minimum of 3 hours so that it becomes firm.
- Serve as a mound with dark bread (and beer if desired).

Nutrition Information

- Calories: 603.2
- Saturated Fat: 36.2
- Fiber: 1.9
- Total Carbohydrate: 7.5
- Cholesterol: 151.7
- Sodium: 874.8
- Sugar: 1.1
- Protein: 16.5
- Total Fat: 57.9

103. Mader's Hungarian Goulash

Serving: 4-5 serving(s) | Prep: 25mins | Ready in:

Ingredients

- 2 lbs onions, sliced
- 1/2 cup oil or 5 ounces lard
- 1 1/2 teaspoons paprika
- 2 lbs beef chuck, cut in 2 inch cubes
- 1 pint beef stock
- 1 1/2 teaspoons tomato paste
- 1 teaspoon salt
- 1 teaspoon vinegar
- 1/2 lemon, rind of, finely chopped
- 1 clove garlic, finely chopped
- 1 teaspoon caraway seed
- water, to thin goulash

Direction

- In large, heavy pot, fry onions in hot oil until golden brown, about 10 to 15 minutes.

- Add paprika and stir well.
- Add meat, cover and let meat brown lightly, stirring frequently.
- Add stock, tomato paste, salt and vinegar.
- With mortar and pestle, or flat part of heavy knife, mash lemon rind with garlic and caraway seeds.
- Add to meat mixture.
- Cover and simmer very gently about 30 minutes, or until meat is tender.
- Add additional water in small quantities if needed.
- Serve with boiled potatoes, noodles or dumplings and a fresh, crisp roll.

Nutrition Information

- Calories: 930
- Fiber: 3.8
- Cholesterol: 156.5
- Protein: 45.5
- Total Fat: 72.3
- Saturated Fat: 21.7
- Sodium: 1129.6
- Sugar: 10.1
- Total Carbohydrate: 24.3

104.   Mary Ann's Goulash

Serving: 6-8 serving(s) | Prep: 10mins | Ready in:

Ingredients

- 1 -1 1/2 lb ground meat
- 8 ounces elbow macaroni
- 1/2 cup chopped green pepper
- 1/2 cup chopped onion
- 1 (14 1/2 ounce) can tomatoes (crushed tomatoes okay) or 1 (8 ounce) can tomato sauce
- salt (to taste)
- pepper (to taste)
- garlic (to taste)

Direction

- Cook elbow noodles until not quite done; drain and set aside.
- Brown the meat with peppers, onions, salt, pepper garlic. Drain if necessary.
- Add tomatoes and elbow noodles. You may also need to add additional water.
- Cook for 15-20 minutes until most of the liquid has cooked down.
- I generally give a taste test and add more salt and probably more powdered garlic.

Nutrition Information

- Calories: 169.9
- Saturated Fat: 0.1
- Sodium: 6.2
- Fiber: 2.5
- Sugar: 3.4
- Total Carbohydrate: 34.7
- Cholesterol: 0
- Total Fat: 0.8
- Protein: 6.1

105.   Mititei

Serving: 36 sausages, 36 serving(s) | Prep: 1hours | Ready in:

Ingredients

- 2 lbs ground pork
- 2 lbs ground lamb
- 2 teaspoons salt
- 7 teaspoons crushed garlic
- 2 teaspoons baking soda
- 2 teaspoons pepper
- 3 teaspoons dried thyme
- 1/2 teaspoon allspice
- 1/4 teaspoon coriander
- 1/4 teaspoon cumin
- 1/2 teaspoon fennel seed
- 1/2 cup stock

- 2 teaspoons lime juice
- 2 teaspoons olive oil

Direction

- The day before you plan to cook, mix the dry ingredients and meats. In a separate bowl combine the wet ingredients, then add just enough of the wet ingredients, to achieve a "hamburger mix" consistency. Retain unused wet ingredients.
- Leave both mixtures covered in the fridge overnight.
- 30 minutes before cooking bring both mixtures out of the fridge and add more wet ingredients to meat mixture if necessary.
- Form breakfast sausage size rolls of the mixture 8 to 10 cm long (3 or 4 inches). Best effects come from grilling over a high charcoal heat.
- Serve with flat bread or pita and some hearty mustard, diced onions and tomatoes to finish a sandwich or with standard BBQ sides and salads.

Nutrition Information

- Calories: 149.9
- Saturated Fat: 4.6
- Sodium: 232.7
- Fiber: 0.1
- Cholesterol: 42.1
- Total Fat: 11.4
- Sugar: 0
- Total Carbohydrate: 0.4
- Protein: 10.7

---

106. Momosita's Borscht

Serving: 8-10 serving(s) | Prep: 15mins | Ready in:

Ingredients

- 4 quarts water

- 1 1/2 lbs stew meat (optional)
- 2 medium onions, sliced into rounds
- 2 stalks celery, cut in 1-inch lengths
- 4 -6 carrots, sliced into thin coins
- 4 beets, peeled and sliced
- 1 head green cabbage, cut into wedges
- 1 bay leaf
- 1 tablespoon salt
- 1 beet, grated (optional)
- 1 (6 ounce) can tomato paste
- 2 tablespoons vinegar
- 1 -2 tablespoon honey
- sour cream

Direction

- Into 4 quarts of water add stew meat, onions, celery, sliced beets, cabbage, bay leaf, and salt.
- Simmer for 3.5 hours.
- After simmering add grated beets (optional), tomato paste, vinegar and honey.
- Simmer for another 20 minutes.
- Add salt and pepper to taste.
- Serve each bowl with a dollop of sour cream.

Nutrition Information

- Calories: 89.9
- Fiber: 5.5
- Sugar: 13.6
- Total Fat: 0.4
- Sodium: 1120.5
- Protein: 3.6
- Saturated Fat: 0.1
- Total Carbohydrate: 21
- Cholesterol: 0

---

107. Moravian Style Sauerkraut

Serving: 4 serving(s) | Prep: 10mins | Ready in:

Ingredients

- 1 (2 lb) bagfranks sauerkraut (or equivalent)
- 4 slices bacon
- 1 medium onion, chopped
- 1 medium potato, grated
- 1 teaspoon caraway seed
- 1 teaspoon flour

Direction

- Drain juice from kraut.
- With kraut still in bag add tap water.
- Pour kraut and water into a saucepan and heat over a low flame.
- Fry bacon, crumble and add to kraut, saving fat for onion.
- Sauté onion in fat till soft and add to kraut.
- Add potato to kraut.
- Simmer for 45 minutes.
- Make a roux by adding flour to bacon fat.
- If too sour add 1 tsp. sugar to kraut.
- Good dining.

Nutrition Information

- Calories: 135.9
- Protein: 4.5
- Total Fat: 4.1
- Sodium: 1571.5
- Fiber: 8.4
- Sugar: 5.6
- Saturated Fat: 1.3
- Total Carbohydrate: 22.4
- Cholesterol: 5.4

108. Muckalicka

Serving: 4 serving(s) | Prep: 5mins | Ready in:

Ingredients

- 1 1/2 lbs boneless pork chops, cut in 1/2-inch X 1/2-inch slices
- 1/2 cup water
- 3 medium onions, sliced into rings

- 2 medium tomatoes, diced in 3/4-inch cubes
- 1 large green pepper, cut into 1/4-inch X 1 1/2-inch strips
- 1/2 teaspoon vegit seasoning
- 1/2 teaspoon Hungarian paprika
- 1 teaspoon salt
- 1/4 teaspoon crushed red pepper flakes
- 1/4 teaspoon ground black pepper
- 1 dash Clamato juice
- 2 ounces feta cheese

Direction

- Mix the spices together in a small container.
- Heat 2 tablespoons cooking oil in large skillet, add pork strips and cook over medium heat until browned, about 15 minutes. Stir often.
- Add water, onions, tomatoes and seasonings. Cover and simmer 30 minutes. Stir occasionally.
- Add green pepper strips and Clamato. Replace cover and simmer an additional 7-8 minutes. Stir occasionally.
- Serve with roast potatoes on the side. Sprinkle each serving with crumbled Feta.

Nutrition Information

- Calories: 357
- Fiber: 3
- Protein: 40.7
- Total Fat: 15.3
- Saturated Fat: 6.5
- Sodium: 840
- Sugar: 6.8
- Total Carbohydrate: 12.9
- Cholesterol: 127.4

109. Mustard Chive Spaetzle

Serving: 4 serving(s) | Prep: 5mins | Ready in:

Ingredients

- 4 large eggs, at room temperature
- 3/4 cup milk
- 3 tablespoons Dijon mustard
- 1 teaspoon salt
- 1 tablespoon snipped chives
- 1/4 teaspoon freshly grated nutmeg
- 2 cups all-purpose flour
- 2 -4 tablespoons unsalted butter, melted (optional)

Direction

- Make sure to read through all steps below before executing this recipe!
- Beat the eggs the next 5 ingredients. This works well with or without the chives and nutmeg if you do not have any.
- Add the flour mix until a sticky batter form. [Note: If your spaetzle is too heavy or dense in the end, then you know for next time that you used too much flour.].
- Bring a pot of salted [generously salted] water to a boil.
- If you have a spaetzle maker, work the batter through the sieve.
- For the rest of us, take a small plastic cutting board and place a decent line/dollop of batter across about 2/3rds of the way up the board. Holding the board at a slight downward angle over the boiling water, very quickly, using a butter knife, scrape off small bits of batter [to make each spaetzle] into the boiling water, dipping the knife into the water with the batter each time [less stickiness]. Don't worry, this takes some practice to do well! Remember, the spaetzles are supposed to be relatively small, but most importantly, even in size as they cook together! After going through this process once, you will also get a better feel for what the proper consistency of the batter should be when adding in the flour in step 3.
- There is also the "colander" method [push batter through colander over boiling pot], however, I've never gotten it to work well and the batter sort of cooks in the holes over the pot before you've worked your entire batter.

Plus, I find they are almost too small this way lose all their satisfying chewiness. Maybe this is all because I grew up making these with my grandma who was a natural spaetzle machine! {By the way, she used a teaspoon rather than a butter knife on the cutting board, which you could try too}.

- They are done when they rise to the top of the boiling water, only about 1 to 2 minutes {why I said "very quickly" earlier}. You may need to do this in batches, especially at first, so that your pot doesn't have overcooked and undercooked spaetzle at the same time. They should be just slightly chewy still when done, but cooked all the way through.
- Drain well.
- At this point, you can serve right away with your meal [they get cold fast], or sauté them in 2-4 tbsp of butter as needed to coat them, stirring constantly.
- Enjoy! Great with dishes that have sauces and gravies to keep them warm on your plate.
- Now that you've read through this, don't be too intimidated and go plan a session to make them!

Nutrition Information

- Calories: 338.7
- Protein: 14.7
- Total Fat: 7.7
- Sodium: 801.1
- Sugar: 0.9
- Total Carbohydrate: 51.2
- Saturated Fat: 2.8
- Fiber: 2.1
- Cholesterol: 217.9

110.   My Favorite Beef Paprika

Serving: 6-8 serving(s) | Prep: 5mins | Ready in:

Ingredients

- 2 lbs round steaks, 1/2 inch thick
- 3 tablespoons flour
- 3 tablespoons vegetable oil
- 2 medium onions, thinly sliced
- 1/2 teaspoon salt, to taste
- 1 cup beef stock
- 1 tablespoon paprika
- 1/2 cup sour cream

Direction

- Cut meat into serving size pieces and coat with flour.
- Reserve remaining flour.
- Pour oil into skillet and brown meat over medium heat for about 5 minutes per side.
- Remove meat.
- Add onions to skillet and cook for about 2 minutes, stirring constantly.
- Stir in salt and remaining flour until blended.
- Gradually stir in beef stock and paprika.
- Bring to a boil.
- Return steaks, reduce heat and simmer 45 minutes or until fork tender, turning once.
- Remove steaks, skim fat from gravy and stir in sour cream until blended.
- Heat through- DON'T BOIL!
- Serve with rice or egg noodles.

Nutrition Information

- Calories: 422.3
- Total Fat: 28.3
- Total Carbohydrate: 7.6
- Cholesterol: 120.3
- Protein: 33.1
- Saturated Fat: 10.1
- Sodium: 444.9
- Fiber: 1.1
- Sugar: 2.4

111. Nokedli / Spetzli

Serving: 4-6 serving(s) | Prep: 10mins | Ready in:

Ingredients

- 2 eggs
- 1/4 teaspoon salt
- 400 g flour
- 1/4-1 cup water
- 2 tablespoons butter or 2 tablespoons olive oil

Direction

- Beat eggs add salt and four mixing into a dough add water until it becomes workable but not runny.
- I have a special nokedli maker from Hungry but my mom would put the dough on a flat plat and using a knife just cut pieces or dollops into boiling salted water. Once the dumplings have come to the top allow them to cook another minute or so and remove with a slotted spoon.
- Add butter or olive oil and serve.

Nutrition Information

- Calories: 451.7
- Fiber: 2.7
- Sugar: 0.5
- Total Carbohydrate: 76.5
- Saturated Fat: 4.6
- Cholesterol: 121
- Protein: 13.5
- Total Fat: 9.2
- Sodium: 223.5

112. Noodles And Pot Cheese (Turos Teszia)

Serving: 4-6 serving(s) | Prep: 2mins | Ready in:

Ingredients

- 1 lb wide egg noodles, uncooked
- 1 lb pot cheese, also called Farmer cheese
- 1/2 lb butter
- 1/2 pint sour cream

Direction

- Cook noodles in boiling salted water for about 8 minutes; drain and rinse with cold water.
- Melt 2 tablespoons of the butter in a pan and add the noodles, place over a slow fire, heat well.
- Mix in the cheese and add the sour cream; serve hot.

Nutrition Information

- Calories: 967.7
- Total Carbohydrate: 83.7
- Cholesterol: 243.1
- Saturated Fat: 38
- Fiber: 3.8
- Sugar: 2.3
- Total Fat: 63.1
- Sodium: 381.3
- Protein: 18.4

113. Nutella Palacsinta (Hungarian Crepes With Nutella Filling)

Serving: 8 crepes, 4 serving(s) | Prep: 5mins | Ready in:

Ingredients

- 1/2 cup all-purpose flour
- 2 large eggs
- 1 pinch salt
- 1 cup milk
- 1 teaspoon orange extract
- cooking spray
- 8 tablespoons nutella
- powdered sugar (to garnish)

Direction

- Whisk all ingredients together (except cooking spray) in large bowl till it's smooth. Use electric mixer it is way easier and faster.
- Spray frying pan and heat on medium-high.
- Scoop about 1/4 cup of batter each time.
- Move your frying pan around so the batter could cover the whole bottom.
- Fry it about 3 minutes in the meantime with your spatula go around the edges.
- Flip it with spatula or in the air. Cook about another 2 minutes, then transfer on to plate.
- Spread 1 tbsp. of Nutella all over and roll up.
- Repeat with every crepes.
- Sprinkle powder sugar over them.
- Enjoy!

Nutrition Information

- Calories: 335.9
- Total Fat: 15.9
- Saturated Fat: 4.2
- Fiber: 2.4
- Sugar: 20.7
- Total Carbohydrate: 38.1
- Sodium: 119.2
- Cholesterol: 114.3
- Protein: 8.8

114. Old World Hungarian Goulash

Serving: 8-10 serving(s) | Prep: 20mins | Ready in:

Ingredients

- 1 tablespoon butter
- 1 1/2 lbs ground beef
- 1 large red onion, diced
- 1 (14 1/2 ounce) can beef broth
- 1 (6 ounce) cancan tomato paste
- 2 (14 1/2 ounce) cans crushed tomatoes
- 3 garlic cloves, chopped

- 1 tablespoon Worcestershire sauce
- 1 tablespoon paprika
- 1 teaspoon salt
- 1 teaspoon pepper
- 1 teaspoon season salt
- 1/8 teaspoon liquid smoke
- 1 cup cold water
- 3 tablespoons all-purpose flour
- 1 green bell pepper, cut into strips
- 16 ounces elbo macaroni, package, Partially cooked according to directions

Direction

- Heat butter in a large skillet over medium-high heat.
- Cook beef in butter, stirring occasionally, until lightly browned.
- Do not drain.
- Place beef and sliced onion in a slow cooker.
- Mix partially cooked elbow macaroni, beef broth, tomato paste, crushed tomatoes, garlic, Worcestershire sauce, paprika, season salt, liquid smoke, salt, and pepper; stir into beef mixture.
- Cover and cook on low heat 4-5 hours (I always use the longer cook time).
- Mix water and flour; gradually stir into beef mixture.
- Stir in green pepper.
- Cover and cook on high heat 30 minutes. Serve with a dollop of sour cream atop.

Nutrition Information

- Calories: 488.3
- Sugar: 5.6
- Total Carbohydrate: 60.1
- Sodium: 882.8
- Fiber: 5.7
- Cholesterol: 61.6
- Protein: 27.3
- Total Fat: 15.8
- Saturated Fat: 6.2

115. Palocleves

Serving: 4 serving(s) | Prep: 20mins | Ready in:

Ingredients

- 320 g paschal lamb shoulder, cut into 10 x 10 mm dice (1/2 inch)
- 3 tablespoons sunflower oil
- 100 g onions, finely chopped
- 1 teaspoon Hungarian paprika, preferably sweet
- 1 clove garlic, crushed
- 1/4 teaspoon ground caraway
- 1 bay leaf
- salt, to your taste
- 250 g potatoes, cut into 10 x 10 mm dice (1/2 inch)
- 150 g french beans, cut into 20 mm pieces
- 1/2 cup sour cream
- 2 tablespoons plain white flour
- 1 -2 tablespoon dill, finely chopped

Direction

- In a 2 quarts pot fry the onion on the hot oil until golden brown.
- Set aside for a short time, and then mix in the Hungarian paprika, and two cups of hot water.
- Put back on the medium fire, add the meat dices, some salt, caraway, garlic and bay leaf, reduce the heat, and on slow fire simmer covered for about 1 and the half hours, or until the meat is tender.
- Continuously add water if needed.
- While the meat simmers in a small pot boil the diced potatoes in some salted water (about 10-12 minutes), then set aside.
- Boil the French bean pieces in a cup of salted water (about 10-12 minutes) and set them aside too.
- Do not overcook the bean!
- If you use green beans, add some bicarbonate of soda to the water to keep the fresh green color of the bean.

- In a small bowl mix well the sour cream and the flour with 1/4 cup of water using a whisk.
- When the meat is tender, add the potatoes and the bean with the simmering water, then mix in the sour cream thickening and simmer another 5 minutes.
- If you think that the soup is too thick, mix in some hot water.
- Before the serving, discard the bay leaf, and sprinkle every serving with spoonful fresh, finely chopped dill.

Nutrition Information

- Calories: 438.9
- Cholesterol: 70.2
- Saturated Fat: 12.5
- Sodium: 69
- Fiber: 2.1
- Sugar: 1.7
- Total Fat: 33.6
- Total Carbohydrate: 18.3
- Protein: 16.2

116.   Paprikas Burgonya (Paprika Potatoes)

Serving: 4 serving(s) | Prep: 30mins | Ready in:

Ingredients

- 1 small onion, finely chopped
- 2 tablespoons butter
- 1 teaspoon paprika
- 6 sliced potatoes
- salt

Direction

- Sauté finely chopped onion in butter.
- Add paprika when onions are lightly browned; then add potatoes and salt.

- Cover and keep stewing, adding enough water to keep potatoes from sticking. Turn now and again with pancake turner.
- Simmer until potatoes are soft.
- Before serving add a little sour cream, if desired.

Nutrition Information

- Calories: 305.8
- Saturated Fat: 3.8
- Fiber: 7.5
- Total Carbohydrate: 57.9
- Cholesterol: 15.3
- Protein: 6.8
- Total Fat: 6.1
- Sodium: 60.8
- Sugar: 3.3

117.   Parslied Egg Noodles

Serving: 6 serving(s) | Prep: 10mins | Ready in:

Ingredients

- kosher salt
- 1 (12 ounce) package wide egg noodles
- 4 -6 tablespoons cold unsalted butter, cut into bits
- 3 tablespoons flat leaf parsley, chopped
- fresh ground black pepper

Direction

- Bring a large pot of water to a boil over high heat and salt generously.
- Add the noodles and cook, stirring occasionally, until al dente, about 5 minutes.
- Ladle 1/4 cup of the noodle cooking water into a medium skillet. Whisk in the butter bit by bit over low heat, letting each piece melt completely before adding the next, to make a creamy sauce.

- Stir in the parsley and season with salt and pepper.
- Drain the noodles, toss with the sauce, and serve immediately. Enjoy!

Nutrition Information

- Calories: 287.4
- Saturated Fat: 5.5
- Sodium: 14
- Total Carbohydrate: 40.8
- Cholesterol: 68.2
- Total Fat: 10.2
- Fiber: 1.9
- Sugar: 1.1
- Protein: 8.2

---

118.   Peach Ketchup

Serving: 4 cups | Prep: 30mins | Ready in:

Ingredients

- 1 tablespoon vegetable oil
- 1 onion, thinly sliced
- 5 peaches, pitted,peeled and roughly chopped
- 1/2 cup white vinegar
- 1/4 cup light brown sugar
- 3 tablespoons molasses
- 2 tablespoons sugar
- 1 teaspoon salt
- 1/2 teaspoon cracked black pepper
- 1/2 teaspoon garlic powder
- 1/4 teaspoon allspice
- 1 lemon

Direction

- Heat oil in large saucepan over medium heat.
- Add onion and cook until transparent.
- Add peaches and cook 4 minutes, stirring often.
- Add vinegar, brown sugar, molasses, sugar, and spices.

- Reduce heat to simmer and cook 1 hour, stirring occasionally.
- If necessary, add small amount of water to prevent the mixture from sticking or burning.
- Remove from heat.
- Add the juice of 1 lemon.
- Put into blender or food processor and puree.
- Serve at room temperature.

Nutrition Information

- Calories: 222.9
- Fiber: 3.6
- Cholesterol: 0
- Saturated Fat: 0.5
- Sodium: 595.7
- Sugar: 39.5
- Total Carbohydrate: 49
- Protein: 1.8
- Total Fat: 3.9

---

119.   Peppy Paprika Potatoes

Serving: 4 serving(s) | Prep: 10mins | Ready in:

Ingredients

- 2 lbs russet potatoes (about 4-6 potatoes peeled and cut in large cubes)
- 1 onion, halved and sliced
- 2 -4 garlic cloves, minced
- 2 tablespoons olive oil (or to coat)
- 1/2 tablespoon hot paprika
- 1/2 teaspoon coarse salt
- 1/2 teaspoon pepper
- 1 lemon juice
- 1 tablespoon butter

Direction

- Preheat oven to 350 degrees.
- Toss all but the butter together and place in a casserole dish.
- Top with butter.

- Place in oven for 30 minutes uncovered.
- Toss all and bake for 30 more minutes at 400 degrees.
- Garnish with additional salt and lemon if desired.

Nutrition Information

- Calories: 278.9
- Sugar: 3.4
- Cholesterol: 7.6
- Protein: 5.2
- Saturated Fat: 2.9
- Fiber: 5.9
- Total Fat: 10
- Sodium: 331.9
- Total Carbohydrate: 44.2

---

120. Pigs In The Blanket Aka Stuffed Cabbage

Serving: 24 cabbage rolls, 10-12 serving(s) | Prep: 30mins | Ready in:

Ingredients

- 2 lbs lean ground beef
- 1 lb pork sausage
- 1 1/2 tablespoons garlic salt
- 1 tablespoon sweet paprika
- 1/2 teaspoon black pepper
- 2 cups white rice, cooked and cooled
- 1 large cabbage
- 2 (28 ounce) cans whole canned tomatoes, crushed with a fork
- 32 ounces chicken broth (organic or homemade is best)
- olive oil, to coat roasting pan
- salt and pepper

Direction

- Wilt head of cabbage in large pot of boiling water for 5 minutes. Remove cabbage from pot, cool slightly and separate leaves, taking care not to break the leaves.
- Mix ground beef, sausage, cooked rice, garlic salt, paprika and pepper. Form 3 inch balls. Place meatball into cabbage leaf and fold leaf around the ball. Place roll into a large square of cheesecloth, cover and twist ends of the cloth to shape and tighten the roll. Remove cabbage roll and repeat until all filling is used.
- In a large roasting pan which has been coated with olive oil, place layer of cabbage rolls (folded side down), cover with 1 can of tomatoes, and repeat. Pour chicken broth over the layers.
- Preheat oven to 325 degrees F. Cover roasting pan and bake for 2 hours or until cabbage is tender. Serve with mashed potatoes.

Nutrition Information

- Calories: 515.6
- Fiber: 6.2
- Protein: 32.7
- Total Carbohydrate: 45.7
- Cholesterol: 91.7
- Total Fat: 22.3
- Saturated Fat: 8
- Sodium: 902.5
- Sugar: 8.2

---

121. Pineapple And Cheese Lattice Squares

Serving: 16-20 serving(s) | Prep: 1hours | Ready in:

Ingredients

- Filling 1
- 1/2 cup sugar
- 3 tablespoons cornstarch
- 1/4 teaspoon salt
- 1 egg yolk
- 1 2/3 cups canned crushed pineapple with juice
- Filling 2

- 1 lb cottage cheese
- 1 egg yolk
- Dough
- 2/3 cup milk
- 1 teaspoon sugar
- 1 (1/4 ounce) package dry active yeast
- 1/4 cup lukewarm water (105 degrees)
- 4 egg yolks
- 4 cups flour
- 1 cup cold butter, cut into small cubes

Direction

- Mix 1/2 cup sugar, cornstarch, and salt in a sauce pan.
- Stir in 1 egg yolk and pineapple.
- Cook over medium-medium-high heat until think.
- Set aside to cool completely.
- In a medium bowl, mix together cottage cheese and 1 egg yolk and set aside.
- Scald milk
- Add teaspoon of sugar to milk and set aside to cool to lukewarm.
- Dissolve yeast in lukewarm water for 1-2 minutes.
- Add yeast mixture to milk and set sit until lots of little bubbles form on surface.
- In a large bowl cut together butter and flour until in resembles a course meal.
- Stir yeast mixture into the flour mixture
- On a floured surface, roll out 2/3's of the dough to fit the bottom of a 16-10" baking pan.
- Spread cottage cheese mixture over dough followed by pineapple mixture.
- Roll out remaining dough and cut into lattice strips.
- Lay the strips in an over-under pattern across the top of the pineapple mixture to give the lattice effect.
- Cover and let rise in a moist warm area for 1 hour.
- Bake in a preheated oven for 35-40 minutes.

Nutrition Information

- Calories: 317.6
- Total Carbohydrate: 37.4
- Sodium: 242.4
- Sugar: 10.5
- Saturated Fat: 8.9
- Fiber: 1.2
- Cholesterol: 107
- Protein: 8.4
- Total Fat: 15

122. Porcini Potato Latkes

Serving: 10 4 inch latkes, 4-5 serving(s) | Prep: 1hours | Ready in:

Ingredients

- 1/2 ounce dried porcini mushrooms, mushrooms*
- 3/4 cup hot water
- 7 tablespoons olive oil (or more)
- 2 garlic cloves, finely chopped
- 1 teaspoon Hungarian paprika
- 1 1/2 lbs russet potatoes, peeled
- 1 large egg, beaten
- 2 tablespoons fresh breadcrumbs, preferably made from egg bread
- 1 teaspoon salt
- 1/2 teaspoon ground black pepper

Direction

- Place porcini in small bowl. Add 3/4 cup hot water and let stand 45 minutes.
- Strain through fine sieve, reserving soaking liquid. Coarsely chop porcini.
- Heat 1 tablespoon oil in heavy medium nonstick skillet over medium-high heat.
- Add chopped porcini and garlic; sauté 2 minutes. Add reserved porcini soaking liquid and paprika; cook until liquid evaporates, stirring frequently, about 3 minutes.
- Season with salt and pepper.
- Set aside to cool.

- (Mushroom mixture can be made 1 day ahead. Cover and refrigerate.)
- Finely grate potatoes by hand or in processor fitted with grating disk.
- Transfer potatoes to large bowl. Add enough cold water to cover; let stand 5 minutes. Drain potatoes. Wrap in dry kitchen towel; twist ends to squeeze out as much liquid as possible. It is important to have the potatoes dry.
- Place potatoes in large bowl. Mix in egg, breadcrumbs, salt, and pepper. Stir in mushroom mixture.
- Heat 6 tablespoons olive oil in heavy large skillet (preferably cast-iron) over medium-high heat until hot but not smoking.
- Working in batches, drop potato mixture by 1/4 cupfuls into hot oil, spacing apart. Using spatula, flatten each into 4-inch round and cook until crisp and brown, about 4 minutes per side.
- Transfer latkes to paper towels to drain. Add more oil to skillet as necessary and allow oil to get hot before adding more potato mixture.
- Transfer to plates and serve.
- *Available at Italian markets, specialty foods stores and many supermarkets.
- Prep time includes soaking time for mushrooms and potatoes.

Nutrition Information

- Calories: 385.7
- Sodium: 634.5
- Fiber: 4.6
- Sugar: 2.5
- Total Carbohydrate: 35.7
- Protein: 6
- Saturated Fat: 3.8
- Cholesterol: 52.9
- Total Fat: 25.3

123.   Potato Romanoff

Serving: 8 serving(s) | Prep: 10mins | Ready in:

Ingredients

- 2 tablespoons chicken soup powder
- 1 teaspoon white pepper
- 1/2 teaspoon garlic salt
- 1/2 teaspoon garlic powder
- 1 tablespoon chives, sliced
- 1/4 cup paprika
- 1/2 cup asiago cheese
- 3/4 cup red onion
- 1 cup cheddar cheese
- 4 ounces cottage cheese
- 4 ounces sour cream
- 1 (1 lb) bag frozen hash browns

Direction

- Combine everything but potato in a bowl and let sit at room temp 15-20 minutes.
- Then cover that bowl and refrigerate overnight, while potatoes are thawing in a colander overnight too.
- Next morning mix potato and cheese mixture together and let sit at room temp for 15-20 minutes.
- Either freeze it (if you're going to use it later) or make it right away.
- 350 degrees for 30-40 minutes.

Nutrition Information

- Calories: 246.2
- Protein: 8.4
- Fiber: 2.7
- Sugar: 2.1
- Total Carbohydrate: 21
- Cholesterol: 23.7
- Total Fat: 15.5
- Saturated Fat: 8
- Sodium: 178.4

124. Pressure Cooker Russian Sweet Sour Cabbage Soup

Serving: 6 serving(s) | Prep: 15mins | Ready in:

Ingredients

- 1/4 cup oil
- 4 tablespoons butter or 4 tablespoons margarine
- 1 onion, thinly sliced
- 4 cups grated red cabbage
- 4 cups grated white cabbage
- 2 cloves garlic, minced
- 1/2 cup seedless raisin
- 1/2 cup dark brown sugar
- 1 teaspoon caraway seed
- 2 quarts chicken stock
- 1 cup dry white wine
- 1/4 cup cider vinegar

Direction

- Heat oil and butter in pressure cooker, just until butter foams.
- Add onion cabbage, stirring until cabbage is wilted.
- Add the remaining ingredients.
- Cover with pressure cooker lid.
- Set on high heat until the control jiggles.
- Reduce the heat and cook for 10 minutes.
- Remove from heat and let cool 5 minutes.
- Run cold water over cooker to finish reducing pressure.
- Serve with sour cream if desired.

Nutrition Information

- Calories: 442.3
- Total Fat: 20.9
- Sodium: 547
- Total Carbohydrate: 48.9
- Cholesterol: 29.9
- Saturated Fat: 7.1
- Fiber: 3.2
- Sugar: 35

- Protein: 10.4

125. Quick Hungarian Goulash

Serving: 4 serving(s) | Prep: 5mins | Ready in:

Ingredients

- cooking spray
- 1 lb lean ground beef
- 1 medium onion, thinly sliced
- 1 medium green pepper, coarsley chopped
- 1 1/2 cups water
- 1 (14 1/2 ounce) can diced tomatoes
- 1 (8 ounce) can tomato sauce
- 1 tablespoon paprika
- 1 teaspoon sugar
- 1/2 teaspoon salt
- 1/2 teaspoon caraway seed
- 4 1/2 ounces rotini pasta, uncooked (I use Tinkyada rice pasta)

Direction

- Spray a 12-inch skillet and heat over medium-high heat.
- Add ground beef, onion and green pepper; cook and stir 5 minutes or until browned.
- Add water, tomatoes, tomato sauce, paprika, sugar, salt, and caraway seed.
- Mix well and bring to a boil.
- Add rotini.
- Reduce heat to medium; cook uncovered for 10-15 minutes or until rotini is tender stirring occasionally.

Nutrition Information

- Calories: 391
- Sodium: 893.7
- Fiber: 5
- Sugar: 9.9
- Protein: 29.2

- Total Fat: 12.5
- Cholesterol: 73.7
- Saturated Fat: 4.8
- Total Carbohydrate: 40.9

126.   Quick Hungarian Sweet Sour Soup

Serving: 6-8 serving(s) | Prep: 5mins | Ready in:

Ingredients

- 2 (16 ounce) cans beef broth (or homemade)
- 1 lb sauerkraut
- 4 -5 tablespoons orange marmalade
- 2 tablespoons ginger preserves (Wilkin Sons is brand label)
- 1 (16 ounce) cansliced red beets

Direction

- Combine all ingredients.
- Heat and serve.

Nutrition Information

- Calories: 125.7
- Total Carbohydrate: 23.9
- Protein: 5.9
- Total Fat: 1.8
- Fiber: 4.2
- Cholesterol: 1.5
- Saturated Fat: 0.1
- Sodium: 1740.5
- Sugar: 17.7

127.   Rizskoch (Hungarian Rice Pudding)

Serving: 10-15 slices, 10 serving(s) | Prep: 20mins | Ready in:

Ingredients

- 1 cup rice
- 250 ml water
- 250 ml milk
- 1 lemon, rind of
- 100 g sultanas
- 6 eggs, separated
- 250 g sugar
- 100 g butter
- 1 -2 teaspoon vanilla sugar
- 50 -60 g butter (butter)
- breadcrumbs

Direction

- Preheat oven to around 200 degrees Celsius.
- Grease a cake tin with extra butter and breadcrumbs.
- Boil rice in water and milk mixture until tender.
- Drain well and add lemon rind.
- Add sultanas and mix. Allow to cool.
- Beat egg yolks with sugar and 100 butter until it is a creamy color.
- Beat egg whites with vanilla sugar.
- Combine with rice and egg yolk mixture.
- Bake in oven for 40-45 minutes or until golden brown and baked through.

Nutrition Information

- Calories: 362.6
- Fiber: 0.7
- Sugar: 31
- Cholesterol: 147.1
- Protein: 6.3
- Total Fat: 16
- Saturated Fat: 9.2
- Sodium: 162.8
- Total Carbohydrate: 49.8

128. Romanian Chilli

Serving: 6 , 6 serving(s) | Prep: 5mins | Ready in:

Ingredients

- 2 tablespoons olive oil
- 1 onion, diced
- 2 green bell peppers, diced
- 2 tablespoons chili powder
- 1 1/2 lbs ground red meat (beef, venison, elk, boar, etc)
- 1 1/2 cups tomato sauce
- 2 garlic cloves, peeled and crushed
- 1 teaspoon dried marjoram
- 1 teaspoon dried sage
- 14 ounces kidney beans, drained and rinsed
- salt and pepper
- coarsely chopped chile (to garnish)

Direction

- Heat oil in a large skillet.
- Add onion and fry on high heat until it begins to turn translucent (2-5 minutes). Stir to prevent burning.
- Add bell peppers and fry another 3 minutes. Keep stirring frequently.
- Add the chilli powder and ground meat. Season with salt and pepper. Keep frying and stirring until meat is browned.
- Add tomato sauce, spices, and kidney beans. Bring to the boil and then simmer 15 minutes, or until beans are soft.
- Garnish with the coarsely chopped chillies.

Nutrition Information

- Calories: 135
- Total Fat: 5.5
- Fiber: 6.5
- Sugar: 5.8
- Total Carbohydrate: 18.2
- Protein: 5.2
- Saturated Fat: 0.8
- Sodium: 562.8
- Cholesterol: 0

129. Roolash

Serving: 4-6 serving(s) | Prep: 20mins | Ready in:

Ingredients

- 1 kg kangaroo fillet, diced
- 1 kg potato, diced
- 1 brown onion, finely chopped
- 2 yellow chilies, sliced
- 2 tablespoons sweet paprika
- 1 tablespoon hot paprika
- 1 teaspoon caraway seed
- 1 teaspoon salt
- 80 ml olive oil
- 1 tomatoes, diced
- 1 (440 ml) can Guinness stout
- 500 ml Coke
- 3 garlic cloves

Direction

- Dice the kangaroo and wack it in a plastic container with the 440ml can of Guinness and the coke, give it a good stir/shake and leave it to marinade overnight.
- Remove the Kangaroo from the marinade, and retain the liquid.
- Place the oil, onion and garlic in the oil and fry till golden.
- Add in the hot paprika and 1 TBS of sweet, the carraway seeds, salt and kangaroo to the pan.
- Add 1 cup of the marinade and 1 cup of water and stir to mix.
- Once it starts to bubble, cover and turn the heat to low and simmer for 1.5 hrs.
- Place in rest of the ingredients in to the pan. If the liquid levels seem more then add more liquid with a 1:1 mix of marinade mix + water. I put in an extra ½ cup of each at this stage.
- Once the spuds are tender, you are done and it's ready to serve.

Nutrition Information

- Calories: 1017.7
- Total Fat: 18.4
- Saturated Fat: 2.6
- Total Carbohydrate: 113.7
- Sodium: 661.9
- Fiber: 8.8
- Sugar: 17.1
- Cholesterol: 0
- Protein: 13.3

---

130.   Salmon Barbecue Marinade

Serving: 12 serving(s) | Prep: 5mins | Ready in:

Ingredients

- 1/2 lb butter
- 2 garlic cloves
- 1/4 cup soy sauce
- 2 tablespoons Dijon mustard
- 1 tablespoon Worcestershire sauce
- 2 teaspoons ketchup

Direction

- Blend all ingredients over low heat.
- Cover fillet (leave skin on one side) and let stand at room temperature for 4 hours.
- When cooking on grill, cook with skin down - use aluminum foil under fillet - DO NOT BURN.

Nutrition Information

- Calories: 143.4
- Protein: 0.9
- Total Fat: 15.4
- Fiber: 0.1
- Total Carbohydrate: 1.2
- Cholesterol: 40.7
- Saturated Fat: 9.7

- Sodium: 495.2
- Sugar: 0.5

---

131.   Smoked Paprika Chicken

Serving: 4 serving(s) | Prep: 10mins | Ready in:

Ingredients

- 2 tablespoons oil
- 1 lb chicken breast, cut into bite sized pieces
- 1 onion, chopped
- 1 garlic clove, minced
- 1 1/2 teaspoons smoked paprika
- 1/2 teaspoon salt
- 1/2 teaspoon black pepper
- 1/2 cup chicken stock
- 1/2 cup sour cream

Direction

- Heat oil in large skillet.
- Add chicken and lightly brown for 5 minutes.
- Add onions and garlic and cook 5 more minutes.
- Season with smoked paprika, salt, and pepper.
- Stir in chicken broth and simmer on low for 10 minutes.
- Remove from heat and stir in sour cream.
- Serve with buttered wide egg noodles.

Nutrition Information

- Calories: 343.5
- Saturated Fat: 7.9
- Total Carbohydrate: 6
- Cholesterol: 86.2
- Total Fat: 23.8
- Sodium: 421.7
- Fiber: 0.8
- Sugar: 1.8
- Protein: 25.8

132. Soft Pretzels Like Auntie Anne's

Serving: 12 pretzels, 12 serving(s) | Prep: 1hours30mins | Ready in:

Ingredients

- 3 1/2 cups flour
- 1 tablespoon sugar
- 1 teaspoon salt
- 1 (1/4 ounce) package dry active yeast
- 1 cup water
- 1 tablespoon Crisco
- 6 cups water
- 1/4 cup baking soda
- 2 tablespoons melted butter

Direction

- Combine 1 cup flour, sugar, salt and yeast in medium bowl. Blend well.
- Heat 1 cup water and Crisco in small saucepan to 100 - 110 degrees.
- Add liquid to flour mixture and blend at low speed until moistened.
- Beat 3 minutes at medium speed.
- Stir in by hand an additional 1-1/2 to 1-3/4 cups of flour or until dough pulls cleanly away from sides of bowl.
- Knead in 1/2 - 3/4 cup flour, on a floured surface, until dough is smooth and elastic.
- Put dough in greased bowl, cover loosely with plastic wrap and a cloth towel.
- Let rise in a warm (80-85 degrees) until light and doubled in size. About 45 minutes.
- Spray 2 cookie sheets with no-stick spray.
- Punch dough down and separate into 12 pieces.
- Roll each piece into a 16-inch rope.
- Form into pretzel shape.
- Place on greased cookie sheets and cover.
- Let rise in a warm place for 15 minutes.
- Adjust oven rack to top position.
- Heat oven to 400 degrees.
- Combine 6 cups water and baking soda in a shallow saucepan and bring to a boil.
- Slowly drop pretzels into water, one at a time, cooking 15 seconds on each side.
- Remove from water with a slotted spoon and return to greased cookie sheet.
- Sprinkle with pretzel salt, sesame seeds, etc.
- Bake for 8 minutes.
- Brush with melted butter.
- Bake an additional 2 minutes or until golden brown.
- Remove from cookie sheet and brush generously with remaining butter.

Nutrition Information

- Calories: 164.9
- Sodium: 1488.7
- Fiber: 1.1
- Total Fat: 3.4
- Total Carbohydrate: 29.1
- Cholesterol: 5.1
- Protein: 4
- Saturated Fat: 1.6
- Sugar: 1.1

133. Sour Cherry Soup

Serving: 4-6 serving(s) | Prep: 15mins | Ready in:

Ingredients

- 2 -3 cups morello cherries in syrup
- 1 -2 teaspoon sugar
- 1/2 lemon, juice of
- 1/2 cinnamon stick
- 500 ml water
- 300 ml thickened cream
- 1 cup sour cream
- 1 teaspoon cornflour

Direction

- Combine Morello Cherries, sugar, lemon juice, cinnamon and water and boil.
- When boiled, reduce heat to a simmer.
- Combine thickened cream, sour cream and corn flour and add to soup through a sieve.
- Cook for a further minute or two until soup thickens.
- Serve chilled.

Nutrition Information

- Calories: 455.3
- Sugar: 17.8
- Cholesterol: 134.1
- Fiber: 2.1
- Total Carbohydrate: 24.6
- Protein: 3.5
- Total Fat: 39.7
- Saturated Fat: 24.2
- Sodium: 81.4

134. Spaetzel

Serving: 6-8 serving(s) | Prep: 10mins | Ready in:

Ingredients

- water or broth, to boil
- 1/2 cup milk
- 1 1/2 cups flour (Sapphire brand is preferred)
- 3 eggs

Direction

- Get a pot of water or broth going at a high boil.
- Mix the milk, flour, and eggs in a bowl. (The resulting batter should be a little thicker than Duncan Hines cake mix; a tiny bit stiff, but definitely not "dough".).
- With a spoon, drop small blobs of batter into the boiling water, and let boil for about 20 minutes. (Be advised that you need to keep the water/broth at a high boil for this to work.

The surfaces of the blobs really need to cook as soon as they hit the water. Then they magically don't stick together. Also, be advised that the blobs will expand as they cook, so try not to make them very large. One way or another, you'll probably have to chop them up with a spatula when you're done anyway.).
- When Spaetzle is done remove it from the broth.
- Drop into Chicken Paprikash when it's done.

Nutrition Information

- Calories: 162.5
- Sodium: 46.1
- Fiber: 0.8
- Cholesterol: 95.8
- Sugar: 0.2
- Total Carbohydrate: 25
- Protein: 7
- Total Fat: 3.4
- Saturated Fat: 1.3

135. Spoon Bread A La Scharf Family

Serving: 8-10 serving(s) | Prep: 20mins | Ready in:

Ingredients

- 3 large onions, in 1/2-inch slices
- 6 tablespoons butter
- 1 cup yellow cornmeal
- 1 cup cream-style cottage cheese
- 1 cup sour cream
- 3 eggs
- 1 teaspoon baking powder
- 1 teaspoon salt
- 1 teaspoon fresh fresh coarse ground black pepper
- 1 teaspoon sugar
- cottage cheese, garnish
- sour cream, garnish

- sugar, garnish

Direction

- Heat oven to 375°F.
- Butter a 2-quart baking dish.
- Add 4 Tablespoons of butter to large sauté pan add onions. Sauté for about 15 minutes until golden, not too brown.
- In a large bowl add cornmeal and moisten with hot water until all the meal is moist but not too wet.
- In a smaller bowl beat the eggs together then add to cornmeal.
- Add the sautéed onions with butter, sour cream, cottage cheese, salt, pepper and sugar.
- Combine all those ingredients together. Mix well. If it still looks dry add the rest of butter or some extra sour cream.
- Put it into a buttered covered baking dish and bake for 45 minutes; remove cover and brown on top, about 10-15 minutes.
- Watch it so it does not burn.
- Spoon bread will be brown and crusty on the outside and soft creamy inside.
- Serve with sugar, sour cream cottage cheese or savory with more black pepper and if desired more salt.
- ENJOY!

Nutrition Information

- Calories: 274.3
- Saturated Fat: 10.7
- Sodium: 552.4
- Cholesterol: 118.8
- Protein: 8.4
- Total Fat: 18.3
- Total Carbohydrate: 20.3
- Fiber: 2
- Sugar: 3.3

136.   Stove Top Hungarian Goulash

Serving: 6 serving(s) | Prep: 20mins | Ready in:

Ingredients

- 2 lbs flank steaks, cut into strips
- 1 green bell pepper, cut into strips
- 2 yellow onions, cut into strips
- 2 garlic cloves, minced
- 2 tablespoons paprika
- 1/2 teaspoon salt
- 1/2 teaspoon Mrs. Dash seasoning mix
- 1/2 teaspoon pepper
- 1 tablespoon butter
- 3 tablespoons olive oil
- 1 (6 ounce) can tomato paste
- 2 cups beef broth
- 1/2 cup sour cream (optional)
- To coat meat
- 1/2 cup flour
- 1/4 teaspoon salt
- 1/8 teaspoon pepper
- 1/4 teaspoon garlic powder
- 1/2 teaspoon paprika

Direction

- Place coating ingredients in a paper lunch bag, or a ziploc bag.
- Shake to mix the ingredients. Add the meat, a few pieces at a time until well coated.
- Add the olive oil and butter to a large, heavy skillet with a lid, and bring to medium high heat. Add meat and cook until well browned. Removed from skillet with a slotted spoon and drain on paper toweling.
- Add onions, peppers and garlic to the skillet (add additional oil or butter if necessary) and sauté until onions are clear. Add meat back to the pan.
- Add remaining ingredients EXCEPT sour cream, and bring to a boil.
- Turn heat to medium low and cover.
- Simmer for 30 minutes, stirring occasionally.

- Remove lid during last five minutes of cooking.
- Stir in sour cream just before serving.

Nutrition Information

- Calories: 420.9
- Saturated Fat: 7.5
- Fiber: 3.4
- Protein: 36
- Total Fat: 22.1
- Sodium: 805.8
- Sugar: 5.8
- Total Carbohydrate: 19.9
- Cholesterol: 67.3

---

137. Sultszalonnas Krumplisalata (Hot Bacon Potato Salad)

Serving: 4 serving(s) | Prep: 1hours | Ready in:

Ingredients

- 8 red potatoes
- 1 small onion
- 1/4 lb bacon
- 3 tablespoons vinegar
- 2 tablespoons flour
- 2 teaspoons sugar
- 1 teaspoon salt
- 1 cup water

Direction

- Cook potatoes in boiling water until tender.
- Peel, cut into slices, and place in mixing bowl.
- Dice and fry in frying pan 1/4 lb. bacon, till almost crisp. Do not let burn.
- Remove diced bacon and place into mixing bowl with other ingredients.
- Peel and dice onion and place into reserved bacon fat. Sauté a few minutes.

- Remove sautéed diced onion with slotted spoon and place into mixing bowl.
- Into at least 2 Tbs. bacon fat, cook 2 Tbs. flour until smooth and bubbly, add 3 Tbs. vinegar and 2 teaspoon sugar, 1 teaspoons salt, and enough water to make a medium sauce. (About 1 cup or more).
- Bring to a boil and cook until sauce is thickened.
- Pour over ingredients in mixing bowl, and toss and mix.
- Taste, if needed add more salt. (Vinegar and Bacon are salty, so add salt last).

Nutrition Information

- Calories: 468.4
- Total Fat: 13.4
- Saturated Fat: 4.4
- Sodium: 845.3
- Fiber: 7.6
- Cholesterol: 19.3
- Sugar: 7.1
- Total Carbohydrate: 74.8
- Protein: 11.9

---

138. Super Chicken Drumsticks Paprika

Serving: 4 serving(s) | Prep: 5mins | Ready in:

Ingredients

- 8 chicken legs
- 1 medium onion, sliced
- 2 teaspoons olive oil
- 2 teaspoons paprika, Hungarian sweet
- 1/2 teaspoon pepper
- 1 teaspoon salt

Direction

- Place onion slices in sprayed slow cooker.

- Arrange chicken legs over top, on one layer as much as possible.
- Combine remaining ingredients with 1 teaspoons water and brush over chicken.
- Cover and cook on low 7-8 hours or until chicken is tender and cooked through.

Nutrition Information

- Calories: 659.7
- Sodium: 846.6
- Cholesterol: 277.2
- Protein: 61.1
- Total Fat: 42.9
- Saturated Fat: 11.7
- Fiber: 0.8
- Sugar: 1.3
- Total Carbohydrate: 3.5

139.   Sweet Sour Vegetarian Golabki (Stuffed Cabbage Rolls)

Serving: 4-6 serving(s) | Prep: 20mins | Ready in:

Ingredients

- 1 large head green cabbage
- FILLING
- 1 large onion, ground
- 1 lb vegetarian beef substitute (or ground veggie burger)
- 1/2 cup uncooked brown rice
- 1 cup mushroom, ground
- 1 slice bread, soaked in milk
- 1 egg
- 1/4 tablespoon ketchup
- 1 teaspoon garlic powder
- 1 teaspoon salt or 1 teaspoon celery salt
- 1/2 teaspoon black pepper
- SAUCE
- 29 ounces Hunts tomato sauce

- 1 cup vegetarian beef (use apple juice instead of water) or 1 cup mushroom broth (use apple juice instead of water)
- 2 tablespoons brown sugar
- 1 lemon, juice of
- 9 gingersnaps, ground fine
- 1 small onion, pierced with clove

Direction

- In a large pot, bring salted water to a boil.
- Plunge cored head of cabbage in the water cooking about 5 minutes on each side, using tongs to turn.
- While cabbage is cooking, prepare other ingredients.
- In a large bowl, mix onion, vegetarian beef, rice, mushrooms, bread w/ milk, egg, ketchup and spices.
- Mix well.
- When cabbage is done, let cool for 5 minutes.
- When ready to use, carefully peel back outer leaves and fill with about 2 Tablespoons of filling.
- Roll the leaves up as you would for a burrito or an envelope, making sure you secure all the filling but not overly tight.
- Carefully place rolls closely together in a large pot, packing them tightly until all the filling is used up.
- Put the onion with cloves in the pot.
- Pour tomato sauce and broth over the rolls and bring to a bubble.
- Lower heat to low and simmer one hour, covered.
- Add lemon juice, brown sugar and ginger snaps gently incorporating into the sauce (use a baster if you need) and let simmer for another 15 minutes.
- Serve.

Nutrition Information

- Calories: 754.2
- Saturated Fat: 17.8
- Fiber: 13.8

- Total Carbohydrate: 77.2
- Total Fat: 44.5
- Sodium: 1884.8
- Sugar: 32.3
- Cholesterol: 102.4
- Protein: 17.6

- Sodium: 131.3
- Sugar: 0.5
- Total Carbohydrate: 5.4
- Total Fat: 3
- Saturated Fat: 1.5
- Fiber: 0.1

140. Thin Pancakes (Palacsinta)

Serving: 12-15 pancakes | Prep: 5mins | Ready in:

Ingredients

- 3 eggs, separated
- 1 cup milk
- 1 tablespoon butter, melted
- 1 teaspoon sugar
- 1/2 teaspoon salt
- 1/2 cup flour

Direction

- Beat eggs separately.
- Add all of the remaining ingredients to the egg yolks.
- Beat until smooth (I used a whisk).
- Fold in beaten egg whites.
- Spoon about 3 Tablespoons of batter onto hot greased skillet (I use a 6-inch non-stick skillet and spray cooking spray before each new pancake).
- Tilt the skillet back and forth to spread the batter to the edges of the skillet.
- Brown lightly on both sides, turning with a spatula.
- Serve with jam or cottage cheese, roll, and serve hot.

Nutrition Information

- Calories: 60.2
- Cholesterol: 58.3
- Protein: 2.8

141. Tojasos Krumpli (Egg And Sour Cream Potatoes)

Serving: 6 serving(s) | Prep: 1hours | Ready in:

Ingredients

- 6 large potatoes
- 1/4 lb butter
- 5 eggs
- 1/2 pint sour cream
- 1/2 cup milk
- 3 slices bacon (optional)

Direction

- Preheat oven to 350 degrees Fahrenheit.
- Cook, cool, peel and slice potatoes.
- Place in a large casserole dish and top with dots of butter.
- Salt and pepper to taste.
- Beat the remaining ingredients together, except the bacon, and pour over the potatoes.
- Place the strips of bacon over the top, if desired (These guys were working in minus degree weather and needed those extra calories).
- Bake for one hour and serve while hot.

Nutrition Information

- Calories: 576.1
- Saturated Fat: 16.6
- Sodium: 219.7
- Fiber: 8.1
- Cholesterol: 236.6
- Protein: 14.7

- Total Fat: 28.6
- Sugar: 3.3
- Total Carbohydrate: 67.4

142. Tomato Vodka Soup

Serving: 6 serving(s) | Prep: 30mins | Ready in:

Ingredients

- 2 tablespoons olive oil
- 2 tablespoons unsalted butter
- 2 onions, chopped
- 2 garlic cloves, minced
- 2 tablespoons tomato paste
- 1 (28 ounce) can plum tomatoes, with juice
- 4 cups chicken broth or 4 cups vegetable broth
- 1/2 teaspoon salt
- 1/4 teaspoon fresh ground black pepper
- 1 cup whipping cream
- 1/4 cup vodka
- 1 tablespoon fresh lemon juice
- garlic-flavored croutons (preferably homemade)

Direction

- In a large soup pot, heat oil and butter over medium heat.
- Add onions and garlic; sauté until softened, about 6 minutes.
- Add in tomato paste and sauté until paste turns a rusty brown, about 5 minutes.
- Add in tomatoes with juice, stock, salt, and pepper; bring to a boil.
- Decrease heat and simmer for 40 minutes.
- Using an immersion blender, or in a food processor or blender, in batches, puree soup until smooth.
- Return to the pot, if necessary, and reheat over medium heat until steaming.
- Stir in cream, vodka, and lemon juice.
- Taste and adjust seasoning with salt and pepper, if necessary.

- Ladle into heated soup bowls and garnish with croutons.

Nutrition Information

- Calories: 303.3
- Sodium: 758
- Fiber: 2.5
- Sugar: 6.3
- Protein: 6
- Total Fat: 24.3
- Total Carbohydrate: 11.9
- Cholesterol: 64.5
- Saturated Fat: 12.5

143. Transylvanian Cabbage Gulyas

Serving: 4-6 serving(s) | Prep: 30mins | Ready in:

Ingredients

- 2 small garlic cloves, minced
- 2 medium onions, finely chopped
- 3 tablespoons oil
- 3 slices bacon, diced
- 2 lbs pork, cut into 1/2-inch cubes
- 2 tablespoons paprika
- 1 teaspoon salt
- 1/4 teaspoon caraway seed
- 2 lbs sauerkraut
- 1/2 lb smoked sausage, sliced
- 8 ounces sour cream

Direction

- Peel and chop onions. In large cooking pot place diced bacon and oil. Sauté onions and garlic for 5 minutes over low heat, stirring frequently until onion is light golden.
- Take cooking pot off heat, add paprika and mix well. Place cubed pork on paprika/onion mixture and turn pieces around to coat well. Cook over low heat for a few minutes, stirring

continuously, making sure that paprika does not burn.

- Add salt, pepper, and caraway and mix well. Immediately after, add enough water to cover meat. Cover pot and simmer meat for 45 minutes. While meat is cooking, wash out sauerkraut under cold running water. Squeeze dry and set aside (not necessary if sauerkraut is not too sour) add sauerkraut to meat and cook together until meat is done, about 15 minutes longer. Before serving, add sliced sausage and sour cream. Gently stir into gulyas and cook on low heat for another 2-3 minutes. Serve at once but this dish is better when prepared a day ahead. Sour cream should only be added before serving.

Nutrition Information

- Calories: 1076.7
- Cholesterol: 271.5
- Saturated Fat: 26.2
- Fiber: 7.8
- Total Carbohydrate: 21.6
- Protein: 86
- Total Fat: 71.2
- Sodium: 3245.2
- Sugar: 6.9

---

144.   True Hungarian Chicken Paprikas

Serving: 8 serving(s) | Prep: 1hours | Ready in:

Ingredients

- 2 (3 lb) frying chicken, cut up
- 3 tablespoons butter
- 2 large onions, peeled and chopped
- 2 garlic cloves, crushed
- 2 teaspoons Hungarian paprika
- 1 1/2-2 cups chicken broth
- 1 teaspoon salt (to taste)
- pepper (to taste)
- 2 -3 tablespoons flour
- 2 cups sour cream, at room temperature
- 1 pint heavy cream

Direction

- Wash and cut up chickens into pieces. Heat butter in large skillet and fry chicken pieces till browned. Remove from skillet and keep warm. Pour off most of fat from skillet and add chopped onions and garlic, sauté till tender, add paprika and cook for a minute, add salt and pepper to onion mixture. Add chicken broth and stir well to remove mixture from bottom of pan. In a large Dutch oven or cooking pot, add broth mixture and bring to a boil, add chicken. Make sure there is enough liquid to just cover all the chicken (if there is not enough, then add some water or more broth.) Cook covered on low heat till chicken is so tender it will fall off the bones. Remove chicken to a platter when fully cooked. Combine flour and sour cream, mix into the pot, cook slow, stirring often until thickened and smooth. At this point if sauce is not thick enough, add cream slowly while still cooking on low until desired thickness. You want to achieve a sauce that is a consistency of gravy, but not too thick. Once this is done you will need to make some dumplings as follows:
- 3-C. flour.
- 5 eggs.
- 2 teaspoons salt.
- 1/4 C water.
- Mix ingredients together until smooth. Drop batter by teaspoons into boiling salted water. Cook 10 minutes. Drain. Rinse with cold water. Serve on plates and top off with sauce and chicken. This can also be served with the traditional Hungarian Cucumber salad.
- Hungarian Cucumber Salad with Sour Cream:
- 2 cucumbers.
- 1 lg clove garlic, pressed.
- 1 1/2 teaspoons salt.
- 2 T. vinegar.
- 1/2°C sour cream.
- Hungarian Paprika.

- Pare cucumbers and slice into thin slices, place in bowl, add garlic, toss with salt. Refrigerate for 2 hours. Drain cucumbers very well. Blend vinegar with sour cream and add cucumbers, mix well and sprinkle top with paprika generously, and serve.

Nutrition Information

- Calories: 1118.7
- Sodium: 777.7
- Fiber: 0.9
- Sugar: 3.9
- Total Carbohydrate: 9
- Total Fat: 89.3
- Saturated Fat: 37.8
- Cholesterol: 378.2
- Protein: 67.5

145.   Veal Chops Paprikash

Serving: 4 serving(s) | Prep: 25mins | Ready in:

Ingredients

- For the Paprika Rub
- 2 teaspoons salt
- 1 teaspoon fresh ground pepper
- 1 tablespoon sweet paprika
- 1 1/2 teaspoons hot paprika
- For Rest of Dish
- 4 loin veal chops, at least 1 1/2 inches thick, trimmed of excess fat (can also use rib veal chops)
- 2 tablespoons olive oil
- 3 shallots, chopped
- 3 ounces white mushrooms, brushed clean, chopped
- 1 teaspoon sweet paprika, plus more for garnish
- 1 cup dry white wine
- 1/2 cup sour cream
- salt, to taste
- fresh ground pepper, to taste

Direction

- To make the rub, in a small bowl, mix together the salt, pepper, and the two paprika. Slash the edges of the chops in 1 or 2 places to prevent curling. Sprinkle the chops all over with the rub. Let stand at room temperature for at least 15 minutes or up to 1 hour, or cover and refrigerate overnight. Bring to room temperature if necessary, before cooking.
- In a large, heavy frying pan, over medium-high heat, heat the olive oil. Add the chops and brown for about 2 minutes on each side. Reduce the heat to medium and cover the pan. Cook until an instant-read thermometer inserted away from the bone registers 145 degrees F (63 C) and the meat is lightly pink when cut into near the bone, 4-5 minutes longer. Transfer the chops to a serving platter and tent loosely with aluminum foil while you make the sauce.
- Pour off all but 1 Tb of the drippings from the pan. Add the shallots, mushrooms, and 1 tsp sweet paprika. Sauté over medium-high heat until the shallots are translucent, 3-4 minutes. Add the wine and deglaze the pan, scraping up any browned bits from the bottom. Cook for 1 minute longer, stirring often. Remove the pan from heat and stir in the sour cream. Season to taste with salt and pepper.
- Transfer the chops to individual plates, spoon the sauce on top, sprinkle with sweet paprika, and serve.

Nutrition Information

- Calories: 399.6
- Sodium: 1291.5
- Sugar: 1.3
- Total Carbohydrate: 8.1
- Cholesterol: 111.4
- Total Fat: 24.7
- Saturated Fat: 9.6
- Fiber: 1.5
- Protein: 26.1

146. Veal Paprika

Serving: 6-8 serving(s) | Prep: 20mins | Ready in:

Ingredients

- 2 lbs veal, cut into thin, even slices
- salt
- fresh ground pepper, to taste
- 3 tablespoons olive oil
- 1 tablespoon butter
- 2 shallots, finely chopped
- 1 tablespoon paprika
- 1/4 cup dry white bordeaux
- 1/4 cup chicken broth
- 1 cup sour cream

Direction

- Cut veal slices into 1/4-inch strips.
- Sprinkle with salt and pepper.
- Heat oil in skillet, add veal and cook quickly over high heat until browned. Transfer to a heated serving dish or casserole.
- Melt butter in the same skillet.
- Add shallots and sauté until tender but not browned. Stir in paprika.
- Add wine and cook until liquid is reduced almost completely.
- Add broth; gradually stir in sour cream.
- Combine sauce and meat; heat but do not let boil.
- Serve with hot buttered noodles.

Nutrition Information

- Calories: 413.8
- Sugar: 0.5
- Cholesterol: 145.9
- Protein: 31.1
- Total Fat: 27.1
- Saturated Fat: 11.4
- Fiber: 0.4
- Total Carbohydrate: 4.3
- Sodium: 192.7

147. Vegan Goulash

Serving: 6-8 serving(s) | Prep: 15mins | Ready in:

Ingredients

- 2 cups onions, diced
- 2 cups carrots, diced
- 2 cups zucchini, diced
- 2 tablespoons olive oil
- 2 tablespoons tomato paste
- 2 teaspoons chili peppers
- 2 tablespoons freshly chopped parsley
- 1/4 teaspoon ground nutmeg
- 2 cups diced tomatoes
- 15 ounces kidney beans (rinsed and drained)
- 15 ounces navy beans (rinsed and drained)
- 1 cup tomato juice
- 1 teaspoon salt
- 1/4 teaspoon ground black pepper

Direction

- In a large pot, sauté the onion, carrot, and zucchini in the olive oil for 5-7 minute Add tomato paste, chili pepper, parsley, and nutmeg. Sauté for 2 minutes. Add remaining ingredients, simmer 15 minutes.
- Serve alone or over pasta, grains, or mashed potatoes.

Nutrition Information

- Calories: 276.3
- Sugar: 11.6
- Total Carbohydrate: 47.5
- Fiber: 14.4
- Sodium: 1137.3
- Cholesterol: 0
- Protein: 12.2
- Total Fat: 5.8
- Saturated Fat: 0.8

148. Veronica's Hungarian Chicken Paprikash/Paprikas

Serving: 4 serving(s) | Prep: 20mins | Ready in:

Ingredients

- 1 chicken, cut up
- salt, to taste
- garlic, to taste
- olive oil, to saute the chicken
- olive oil, to saute the onion
- 1 large onion, chopped
- 1 tablespoon flour
- 1 tablespoon paprika
- 1 cup chicken stock or 1 cup water
- 1 tablespoon tomato paste or 1 tablespoon tomato sauce
- 1 -2 tablespoon sour cream

Direction

- Season the chicken with salt and garlic and sauté in olive oil.
- In a separate pan, sauté the onion in the 1 tablespoons of olive oil until translucent.
- Add the flour, paprika, chicken stock, and tomato paste to the onions and cook, stirring, until sauce thickens.
- Transfer the chicken pieces and the sauce into an oven-proof casserole or baking dish and bake, at 350-400 degrees F., for about 30 minutes, or until chicken is done.
- Just before serving, add the sour cream to the sauce and add more or less sour cream as you like, mixing well.
- Serve with dumplings, mashed potatoes or orzo.
- Bon Appetit!

Nutrition Information

- Calories: 553.7
- Total Fat: 36.3
- Saturated Fat: 10.6
- Sodium: 281.9
- Sugar: 3.2
- Protein: 45.4
- Fiber: 1.4
- Total Carbohydrate: 9.2
- Cholesterol: 175.6

149. Zippy Spices For Flavoring Veggies

Serving: 12 side dishes | Prep: 4mins | Ready in:

Ingredients

- Flavor Mixture
- 4 teaspoons salt
- 2 teaspoons garlic powder
- 2 teaspoons paprika
- 2 teaspoons ground ginger
- 2 teaspoons dry mustard
- Crunch-worthy Add-Ins
- toasted breadcrumbs
- panko breadcrumbs
- butter
- parmesan cheese

Direction

- In a small bowl, combine Flavor Mixture ingredients; store in a small jar with a tight lid.
- Add 1 - 2 teaspoons of Flavoring Mixture (use your own judgment of how much you'd like to add) to your broccoli or cauliflower or asparagus (about a minute before serving, along with some melted butter and a couple hands-full of crumbs. Stir well and finish heating per package instructions.
- I've sprinkled French-fried onions over the top (they don't get crunchy but they add enormous flavor! and that's been met with rave reviews too.
- Sprinkle some parmesan cheese over the top OR another handful of crunchy bread crumbs and serve.

- This mixture (and the toasted crumbs) will jazz up even the most boring frozen veggies-- into something sort-of special.

Nutrition Information

- Calories: 6.2
- Total Fat: 0.2
- Sodium: 775.5
- Total Carbohydrate: 0.9
- Protein: 0.3
- Saturated Fat: 0
- Fiber: 0.3
- Sugar: 0.2
- Cholesterol: 0

---

150.   Zucchini With Sour Cream And Dill

Serving: 4 serving(s) | Prep: 30mins | Ready in:

Ingredients

- 4 medium sized zucchini, sliced thinly
- 2 teaspoons salt
- 3 tablespoons oil
- 1 finely chopped onion
- 2 tablespoons fresh dill or 2 tablespoons dried dill weed
- 1/3 cup sour cream
- 1 teaspoon paprika
- 4 1/2 teaspoons flour
- 3 tablespoons cold water

Direction

- Slice zucchini in thin even slices.
- Sprinkle with salt and stir to distribute evenly. Chill in refrigerator for 1 hour. Drain off the liquid in bottom of the bowl.
- Heat oil and cook onion until softened.
- Add zucchini and dill.
- Cook until crisp tender.

- Stir the sour cream, paprika, flour and water into a smooth a paste; add mixture to the zucchini and cook until the flour has cooked.

Nutrition Information

- Calories: 186.3
- Total Carbohydrate: 12.7
- Protein: 3.6
- Total Fat: 14.7
- Saturated Fat: 3.9
- Fiber: 2.8
- Sugar: 4.7
- Cholesterol: 8.4
- Sodium: 1193.9

Index

Y

L

Conclusion

Thank you again for downloading this book!

I hope you enjoyed reading about my book!

If you enjoyed this book, please take the time to share your thoughts and post a review on Amazon. It'd be greatly appreciated!

Write me an honest review about the book – I truly value your opinion and thoughts and I will incorporate them into my next book, which is already underway.

Thank you!

If you have any questions, **feel free to contact at:** *author@hugecookbook.com*

Demi Decker

hugecookbook.com

Printed in Great Britain
by Amazon